CLEAR TRAUMA NOW

A POWERFUL SOLUTION FOR GETTING UNSTUCK

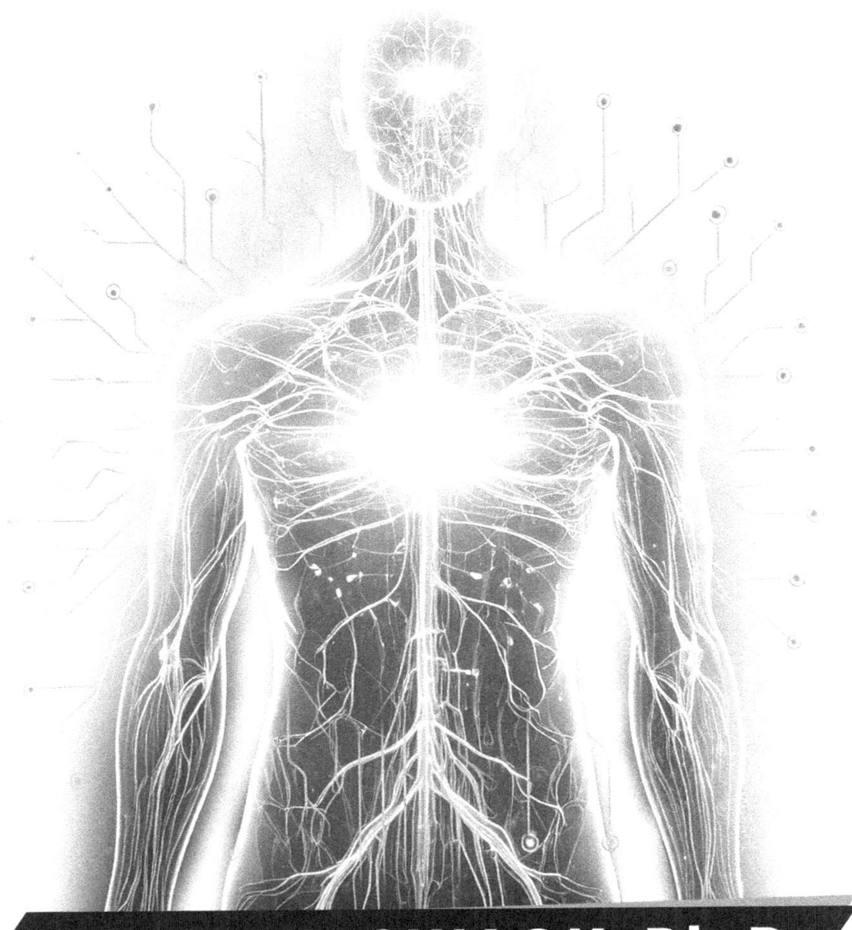

JUDITH A. SWACK, Ph.D.

CLEAR TRAUMA NOW

A POWERFUL SOLUTION FOR GETTING UNSTUCK

JUDITH A. SWACK, Ph.D.

Clear Trauma Now: A Powerful Solution for Getting Unstuck

Published by Brave Healer Productions

Designed by Dino Marino, dinomarinodesign.com

Paperback ISBN: 978-1-961493-84-1
eBook ISBN: 978-1-961493-85-8

Congratulations! You have bought this book to help you clear trauma from every area of your life. As a free gift, I invite you to download this simple two-page worksheet for performing The Simple 4-Step Trauma Clearing Protocol.

https://www.hblu.org/natural-bio-destressing-handout

More free stuff on my website:

https://www.hblu.org/

Sign up for my *free newsletter* containing inspirational articles, healing ideas, and information about upcoming presentations and classes.

You can also sign up for a *free 15-minute consult* with me.

Go here to purchase my Clear Trauma Now with Natural Bio-Destressing video:

https://www.hblu.org/product/Clear-Trauma-Now-with-Natural-Bio-Destressing

In this video (which I think of as "Tap Along with Swack"), I lead you step-by-step through the Natural Bio-Destressing technique, describe the structure of trauma, and give a brief description of the neurobiology of trauma.

Please, please, *please* use these resources to help you, your friends, family, and the whole world stay trauma-free!

Blessings, Judith

DISCLAIMER

The information provided in this book, including text, graphics, and images, is for informational purposes only. It is not to be construed as medical care or medical advice and is not a replacement for medical care given by physicians or trained medical personnel. Neither the author nor the publisher directly or indirectly practices medicine, nor do they dispense medical advice, diagnosis, treatment, or any other medical service as part of this book. Always seek the advice of your physician or other qualified healthcare provider(s) when experiencing symptoms or health problems, or before starting any new treatment. The author and the publisher are not to be held responsible for any inaccuracies, omissions, or editorial errors, or for any consequences resulting from the information provided.

Trigger warning: This book includes real-life examples and case studies of clients who have experienced trauma in many forms, including physical and sexual violence. If you feel triggered by any of these examples, treat yourself with the Natural Bio-Destressing technique right then. Then use the Do-It-Yourself Protocol for Treating Trauma till you feel neutral again. If discomfort persists, use this information to get help from a healing professional.

By continuing to read this book, readers indicate acceptance of these terms.

CONFIDENTIALITY AND GRATITUDE

All the case examples in this book are true stories. I have changed everyone's name (except my own and my family's), sometimes changed their gender, and sometimes combined multiple people into one story to preserve their confidentiality. The purpose of these case examples is to help you recognize similar patterns in yourself and others so you can get the treatment you need to be free of them.

Healing from the Body Level Up™ is a living, breathing healing method that is constantly growing and evolving. I feel I was called by a Divine Source (God) to do this work, and whenever God wants me to discover and heal a new pattern, It sends me several people in a row with the same problem. I feel like I am God's secretary. I research the pattern, take good notes, and then write the protocols for other people to use.

All my clients and colleagues know they're part of the grand experiment to create the best life possible in human form on the planet Earth. They're grateful to benefit from the work of the people who came before them and happy to contribute new experiences and insights to expand the range of what HBLU™ can do. Thank you, God. Thank you, team.

"The Clear Voice Comes Through."

Tribute

Science is never done in a vacuum. Advances in any field are made through collaboration. I'm very grateful to have had (and still have) collaborators and mentors who helped encourage and support the work I've been called to do.

I've used meridian tapping techniques to clear phobias and traumas since Roger J. Callahan, Ph.D., revolutionized the field of psychology when he published his first book on the subject in 1986. When I was ready to publish my research on "The Basic Structure of Loss and Violence Trauma Imprints" in 1994, I asked Roger for permission to reprint a tapping technique in my paper. Not only did he give permission, he was so impressed with my work that he invited me to take his advanced training for free.

In 1997 I got a call from Nathaniel Brandon, Ph.D., another esteemed psychologist and leader in the field of self-esteem. He had read my paper on "The Basic Structure of Loss and Violence Trauma Imprints," thought it was brilliant, and wanted to meet me. He became one of my greatest mentors.

While attending the Association for Comprehensive Energy Psychology (ACEP) Conference in 2017, I met Daniel Benor, M.D., while standing behind him at the copying machine. We instantly recognized each other as kindred scientific research spirits. I became part of his inner circle, and he persuaded (nagged) me to publish some of my other research in his *Journal of Healing and Caring* online.

Roger, Nathaniel, and Daniel: Although you are no longer in the physical realm, the contributions you've made to my life and to the world can never be lost. They live in my work and in my heart. I bless you all every day.

Roger Callahan's work lives on at https://tfttapping.com/
Nathaniel Brandon's work lives on at https://nathanielbranden.com/
Daniel Benor's work lives on at https://www.danielbenor.com/

FOREWORD

Dr. David Gruder

When I first met Judith Swack in 1999, she immediately struck me as a remarkable combination of mad scientist and alchemical healer. Intrigued, I delved into the work she had developed—and quickly discovered that my first impression was accurate. As I explored her system, I found many layers of kinship between our approaches to healing.

Since receiving extensive training from Judith in the early years of our acquaintance, she has often invited me to collaborate, offering input on the interference patterns she uncovers and the treatment methods she continues to refine. Over the decades, I have witnessed her work evolve into something truly extraordinary.

As a clinical and organizational development psychologist whose career has included serving as an administrator for the Association for Holistic Health in the mid-1970s, I've spent decades discerning between valuable healing methodologies and those that are less substantial. As the founding president of the Association for Comprehensive Energy Psychology (1998–2002), and a continuing leader and innovator in the field, I bring a well-honed skepticism to new modalities. My conclusion: Judith's Healing from the Body Level Up™ (HBLU™) framework is pure genius.

If you are already familiar with HBLU™, you are about to discover even deeper layers of its richness. If not, you are standing at the threshold of a system that can unlock profound access to your inner healing resources—and, if you are a helping professional, to support your clients in doing the same.

Here is why this book is so important for humanity:

Early in her career, it became clear to Dr. Swack that unresolved trauma is the most common pattern interfering with people's success in life. Trauma remains one of the most widespread, devastating, and poorly understood problems affecting individuals and societies today. Its imprint embeds deeply into the nervous system, distorting mind, body, and soul functioning—sometimes for a lifetime.

What makes this book particularly valuable is Dr. Swack's original investigations into the precise structure of trauma itself, producing a depth of clarity that remains rare even in advanced trauma work. Pairing this understanding with protocols that are highly effective at clearing trauma imprints from the nervous system produces results that often feel nothing short of magical. The healing process she offers can restore wholeness and vitality even when other approaches fall short.

This book goes beyond only theory to offer practical application. You'll be guided through:

I. A particularly illuminating explanation of the different forms of trauma, including loss, violence, physical injury, surgery, illness, birth trauma, job loss, and more.

II. A scientific discussion of the biochemistry underlying energy psychology methods, thanks to Dr. Swack's extensive background in that field.

III. Innovative protocols to address both acute and chronic trauma—whether self-applied or facilitated by a practitioner.

IV. Simple, learnable techniques that mobilize the body's natural ability to release trauma and restore well-being.

Here is why this book is so important for healing professionals:

- Most helping professionals understand that healing involves both the conscious and subconscious minds, thoughts and feelings. Yet many are missing key components of the puzzle.
- Increasing numbers of practitioners are learning to engage the body-mind connection but still lack essential integration tools.
- Some have explored working with internal "parts"—such as the inner child and inner critic—but have only scratched the surface compared to what HBLU™ offers.
- A growing number address spiritual dimensions alongside psychological and physical healing, but often without a cohesive system to unify their work.
- An expanding field of energy healers works with the biofield, chakras, and meridians—yet many lack an overarching structure to optimize their methods.
- Most who attempt to address these aspects of human experience end up cobbling together disconnected methods, which can be inefficient and incomplete.
- Very few approaches offer a comprehensive, fully integrated framework that addresses all dimensions of human experience in a customized, systematic way.

What if there were a practical, learnable, and well-validated method to integrate all of this? Think of how valuable that would be! Well, guess what? You just struck gold. You have in your hands one of the premiere systems for doing exactly this.

Welcome to the wizarding world of Dr. Judith Swack.

HBLU™ draws upon each individual's deepest wisdom to identify the most appropriate goal for each session, uncover the most relevant interference pattern blocking that goal (very often it is trauma), and determine the optimal treatment method to resolve it. This system brings the body, unconscious mind, conscious mind, and soul into alignment—strengthening inner integration, well-being, and ultimately, one's impact on the world.

HBLU™ is one of the very few methods I've encountered (and I've trained extensively across many healing systems) that succeeds in addressing the full complexity of human healing in a coherent, elegant, and effective way. The result is profound: the ability to actualize your goals free of the baggage that once held you back.

So, put on your wizard's hat, fasten your seatbelt, and prepare to enter HBLU™ World. The gifts you gain will be priceless—for yourself, for those you serve, and for co-creating a more elevated future for humanity.

Dr. David Gruder
Founding President,
Association for Comprehensive Energy Psychology

Author of:

- *Sensible Self-Help: The First Road Map for the Healing Journey*
- *The New IQ: How Integrity Intelligence Serves You, Your Relationships, and Our World*
- *The Nimble C-Suite: How to Align the Diverse Strengths of Your Executive Team to Predictably Deliver Extraordinary Outcomes in a Transformational Economy*

TABLE OF CONTENTS

PROLOGUE

THE GREAT TRAUMA RIPOFF AND THE ACTION PLAN

Janet's husband and the love of her life, Sam, a Marine, committed suicide on an aircraft carrier while at sea. He gave no indication that he was depressed, anxious, or suicidal. Janet wondered out loud, "Was he drinking? Did the Navy cover something up? Was his suicide a side-effect of a vaccine or disease-preventive drug he took for the region of the world he was assigned to? Did he say anything to me in our phone calls that should have alerted me to his state of mind?"

Janet's pain was so intolerable that she started drinking every day, and couldn't sleep without sleeping pills. After a few months, her well-meaning friends and family members encouraged her to "let go and move on." After all, she was still young and had her whole life ahead of her. They were certain she'd marry again.

A few months of unbearable pain later, Janet decided to commit suicide. She drove to the beach at sunset, sat by the waterfront, and downed over-the-counter sleep medications with a fifth of vodka. After she passed out, her body picked itself up and attempted to drive her home. With her conscious mind offline, she drove into a fence. The police arrested her for drunk driving and required her to take a DUI education course, *after which* she came for HBLU™ treatment.

"Why did you wait so long to get help?" I asked. She told me she was afraid to let go of the trauma for fear of losing her husband forever.

This is what I call the *great trauma rip-off.* When someone is traumatized, they can only remember the circumstances around the tragic event, not the positive experiences they had with that person before his/her death. How does this happen?

Phobias and traumas are irrational and exaggerated reactions caused by shocking experiences that trigger the fight/flight/freeze reflex. Anything in the environment at the time becomes associated with the traumatic memory. Later, encountering something that reminds you (even unconsciously) of the original event triggers a "body flashback" to the original memory, causing a phobic reaction.

So, every time Janet thought about her husband, it triggered a picture of him dead in that room, flooding her system with grief and pain. In essence, her husband became equated with trauma, and although she was in pain, she was afraid that letting go of the trauma meant losing her husband.

I explained to Janet, "Only *after* you clear the trauma will you be able to *hold on to and keep the positive memories and feeling*s associated with your husband and experience gratitude for the wonderful contributions he made to your life. Only *after* you clear the trauma will you be able to finish grieving and feel his loving presence." Janet agreed to do the HBLU™ process for clearing trauma.

Since a phobic reaction is a body reflex and can't be controlled consciously, we followed the HBLU™ protocol for clearing trauma using (principally) the Natural Bio-Destressing (NBD) technique (a variation of meridian tapping techniques) to activate the body's own calming reflex (Chapter 8). Activating the calming reflex turns off the fight/flight/freeze reaction, thus eliminating the phobic response. NBD requires no prior experience to learn or use successfully. People focus consciously on the emotional reaction they'd like to clear and then intentionally activate the calming reflex by stimulating specific nerve endings (using tapping with fingertips) on the face, torso, and hands, combined with left brain/right brain integration techniques.

After the first session, Janet could sleep without drugs or alcohol. After the third session, she could spontaneously remember a happy experience with her husband. After the fifth session, Janet knew at the deepest level that she would carry her husband with her and cherish him always, that he would never want her to be unhappy, and that she could go on with her life. With occasional (HBLU™) tune-ups, she was able to move to a new city, find a new job, and date several wonderful men. Five years later, she remarried and eventually had two children.

Whether loss trauma occurred less than a year ago or more than 60 years ago, my clients and I have found that the memory of their loved ones is tainted by trauma unless we use the right techniques to clear it completely at the body, unconscious, conscious, and soul levels. Healing trauma at all levels allows people to easily recall special memories of loving connection and appreciate the ways in which their lives were enriched by having known that person.

Not only does trauma rob people of positive memories of loved ones, it can cause physical illnesses, addictions, and other debilitating reactions and behaviors. Fortunately, after years of research, I found that trauma has a simple and predictable structure. I also found many cutting-edge techniques from the fields of Neuro-Linguistic Programming (NLP) and energy psychology to eliminate traumatic imprints in just a few short sessions. I developed simple and reproducible protocols for healing trauma. Many traumatic experiences can be self-treated, while other traumatic experiences are best treated with the help of trained practitioners.

ACTION PLAN: HOW CAN YOU BEST USE THIS BOOK?

Firstly, it's important that you recognize when you have experienced trauma. Many people recognize that death, divorce, a car accident, physical, sexual, or emotional violence, war, or a terrorist attack are traumatic.

BUT:

- How many teenagers know that a romantic breakup or rejection is traumatic and can lead to suicidal feelings? Even if they did know, how many people who've experienced breakups go for therapy?
- How many people know that illness causes physical injury to the body that causes symptoms later in life (including side effects of vaccines)? And even if they did know, they wouldn't necessarily know what kind of treatment would release those symptoms.
- How many people have had frightening and painful experiences with doctors and dentists, some even causing white coat syndrome (high blood pressure in a doctor's office) or avoidance of necessary medical care? Even if they did know they were traumatized, they probably wouldn't go for therapy.
- How many people know that a job loss can cause anxiety and loss of confidence? How many people who have lost a job go for therapy?

These are just a few examples of traumas you may not have known were traumas. In this book, I give you many examples of common life traumas and the symptoms they cause. I have included a simple HBLU™ protocol for using the Structure of Loss and Violence Trauma outlines combined with the NBD technique to release trauma on your own. I also give you guidelines to know when you need to work with a mental healthcare professional trained in Healing from the Body Level Up™ or other energy psychology or body-centered psychotherapy modalities. Talk therapy has other uses, but doesn't work for clearing trauma.

WHAT THERAPISTS DON'T KNOW, OR KNOW BUT AREN'T WILLING TO TELL YOU

Roger Callahan published his first book on meridian tapping techniques to quickly release phobic reactions from the body in 1985 (1). I published my first paper on "The Basic Structure of Loss and Violence Trauma Imprints" in 1994 (2). In the decades since, there has been a lot of research demonstrating that trauma needs to be healed using a body-oriented psychotherapy approach (3), and extensive research on the efficacy of meridian tapping techniques (4). So why don't therapists know about it, and if they do, why don't they tell you about it and use it to help you?

As often happens when someone brings a revolutionary new improvement to a field, they're violently opposed. Even after Emotional Freedom Technique (EFT), a meridian tapping technique similar to NBD, was approved by the U.S. Department of Veteran's Affairs (VA) as "generally safe" and approved for use, my HBLU™-trained colleagues working as counselors at the VA were forbidden to use it with their clients. The American Psychological Association (APA), to date, refuses to officially recognize energy psychology as a valid form of psychological treatment, even though my colleagues have repeatedly met the research requirements for approval.

Francine Shapiro's work on Eye Movement Desensitization and Reprocessing (EMDR) was first published in 1989 (5). It met resistance for many years and was conditionally approved by the APA in 2017. Although EMDR is effective at clearing trauma from the mind and body, it's only allowed to be used in sessions with a certified practitioner. Colleagues who have trained in both EMDR and meridian tapping techniques tell me they use EMDR and tapping in sessions and teach their clients to do tapping for homework. I have presented this work to large groups of counselors and social workers, and very few train with me. Many of them get treated themselves with HBLU™, but do not use it with their clients.

Don't wait for them! There are many forms of trauma you can treat yourself, and I show you how in Chapter 8 of this book. For traumas that need professional help, find the pioneers, the early adopters, and the lifelong learners who have the curiosity and courage to try new methods themselves, and then offer what works to their clients. I'm still treating clients. You can find advanced HBLU™-trained practitioners on my website (6). You can find energy psychology-trained practitioners on the Association for Energy Psychology website (7). Come train with me.

Take charge of your own life. My purpose for writing this book is to teach you and everyone, lay people and clinicians alike, to recognize the characteristic symptoms of emotional and physical trauma along with a simple technique and protocol to release trauma from body, mind, and soul. With this knowledge, you can now consciously and intentionally free yourself from needless suffering.

INTRODUCTION

THE ORIGIN OF HEALING FROM THE BODY LEVEL UP™ METHODOLOGY

How did a Ph.D. biochemist, immunologist, and research scientist become a mind-body healer? At 30 years old, I had a promising career in biomedical science. I already had a master's degree in biochemical research and was on my way to getting a Ph.D. in biochemistry. I was doing world-class research at the National Cancer Institute, and my love life was a disaster. I kept attracting the same emotionally unavailable man in different bodies. I obsessed, *What am I doing wrong? I'm a smart woman. Why can't I figure this out?*

Then, one of the men I was dating recommended a self-help workshop called Actualizations. In this workshop, I learned about the unconscious mind, which ran 90% of my life and of which I was completely unconscious. Up to that time, as a scientist, I believed the function of the body was to carry around the head. That approach worked well in my scientific career, but not in my love life. I was relieved to realize the problems in my love life were due to damage in my unconscious mind and not some problem with my conscious intelligence. I realized if I wanted to get the desired results in my life, I needed to collaborate with and heal, if necessary, my unconscious mind.

To accomplish this, I needed a new skill set. Stuart Emory, the originator of Actualizations, was trained in Neuro-Linguistic Programming (NLP), a new and highly successful mental technology (as opposed to biotechnology or high technology) designed to help people communicate with and heal their unconscious minds. That year, 1981, I did an NLP practitioner training and began my career as a mind-body healer. My education continued with a Ph.D. in biochemistry, post-doctoral training in human immunology, and Master Practitioner certification in NLP. My personal healing work with other NLP practitioners resulted in the complete disappearance of allergies and asthma, marriage to a wonderful man, a daughter who is the delight of my life, and a career I find very rewarding.

As a scientist, I appreciated the NLP concept that all damage has structure (for example, negative emotions, limiting beliefs, phobias), and that specific damage patterns can be cleared using reproducible protocols. I was also interested in achieving lasting results. If my clients got incomplete results, I asked, "What else is there? Am I looking in the right place for the answer?" Through this quest, I found the body level of healing through the work of Roger Callahan and his Thought Field Therapy, and the work of Mary Louise Muller and her synthesis of applied kinesiology, craniosacral, and polarity therapy. I found the soul level of healing that included ego or personality structure through the work of Andrew Hahn, Psy.D., my Enneagram teacher. I found supernatural interference through the work of many of my clients and colleagues who were versed in religion, shamanism, mysticism, and Jungian psychology. In each of these levels and areas, I collected or created protocols or techniques that worked effectively, and Healing from the Body Level Up™ (HBLU™) was born.

HEALING FROM THE BODY LEVEL UP™ METHODOLOGY

Healing from the Body Level Up™ (HBLU™) is a holistic psychotherapy system that reproducibly clears mental, emotional, physical, and spiritual blocks to success. Developed by Judith A. Swack, Ph.D., HBLU™ integrates the best of biomedical science, psychology, spirituality, applied kinesiology, hypnosis, Neuro-Linguistic Programming (NLP), and other energy psychology techniques with her original research on the structure of complex damage patterns. Thus, HBLU™ is a unique way to get unstuck and eliminate struggle by clearing unconscious patterns that cause self-sabotage. In addition to healing, HBLU™ is a valuable modality for facilitating personal growth, spiritual evolution, and self-actualization. In this chapter I describe the HBLU™ philosophy, the HBLU™ healing process, and how it works.

THE BIG PICTURE: JUDITH SWACK'S PHILOSOPHY AND WORLD VIEW

I believe we all have a soul that is radiant and beautiful. Our souls are currently embodied in human form on the planet Earth. The question is, why?

I believe there are two reasons:

1. We're embodied in order to manifest our soul mission/personal contribution to the world. The ability to manifest our mission is what makes our lives feel meaningful and deeply satisfying. When we die, we can look back on our life and see that the world was a better place for our having been here.
2. We are here to experience the fullness of life and all it has to offer. We're tourists here. This means eat, drink, be merry, learn, love, travel, experience emotional ups and downs, learn about your body and other life-forms on the planet, etc. Life is fascinating!

THE UNITED NATIONS OF SELF

The next question is, what is a human being? In human form, we're a complex mixture of things. Our physical bodies are a symbiotic combination of human cells and bacteria. Bacteria live in our gut, vaginas, sinuses, and skin. Bacteria help us to digest food, make vitamin K for blood clotting, and protect our bodies from disease-causing organisms. We actually could not live without our bacteria! This is why taking broad-spectrum antibiotics that kill our good bacteria, as well as disease-causing bacteria, often results in side effects such as intestinal upset and yeast infections. To counteract this problem, people take bacterial replacement supplements (yogurt, lactobacillus acidophilus pills, etc.) to repopulate their bodies with these protective organisms.

In human form, we're also of several minds, each a different country in language, customs, and values:

- **The conscious mind.** This mind is the land of rational, concrete, linear **logic**. It's very literal. For example, the chair is blue. I have $200 in my wallet.
- **The unconscious mind.** The unconscious mind is the land of **emotion** (which is not rational), imagination, memory, creativity, poetry, and metaphor. It thinks in images, sounds, feelings, tastes, smells, and sensations. It's not literal like the conscious mind. It makes associations and broadens meaning and understanding. For example, the blue chair reminds me of the one we had in our living room that the cat used to sleep on (feeling of happy nostalgia). I have $200 in my wallet and I feel rich. I'm enjoying imagining all the things I could spend it on.
- **The body.** The body is the land of physical survival and reproduction. It values safety, good health, comfort, strength, food, sleep, rest, cleanliness, nurturing touch, sex, etc. The body values providing a good home for the soul so the soul can live in the material world.
- **The soul.** The soul is the land of soul mission and connection with God and all life on this planet and in the universe. The soul values making a contribution and living a full and meaningful life as long as the mortal body lives. The soul knows in order to make a difference in the material plane, it has to become material by living in a body. Souls do not care about reproduction or physical survival. Souls know they're immortal, and when this body dies, the soul can choose to reincarnate in another body, or do something else.

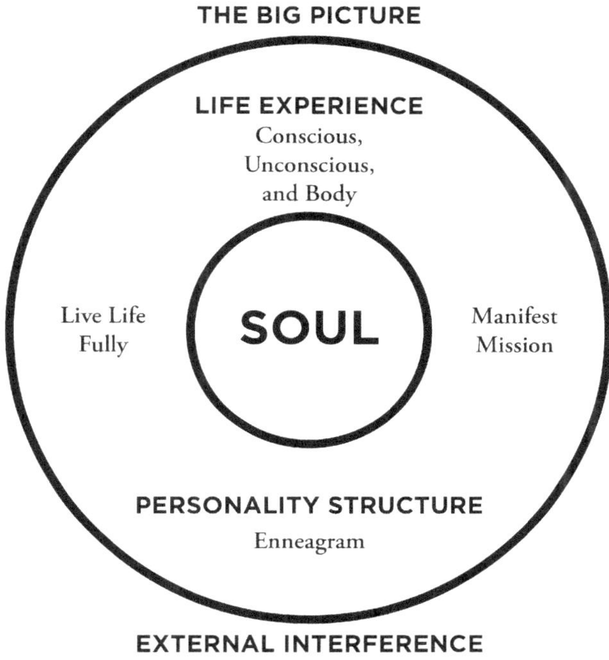

SELF-PEACE, WORLD PEACE

As so often happens between countries, we find ourselves fighting between the different levels of our being. In the United States, we're taught that the conscious mind is the only thing that exists or matters. How then do you explain the common excuse, "I didn't do it on purpose." Which "I" are we referring to?" Remember, we all have a conscious mind, an unconscious mind, a body, and a soul. All of these levels are all "I." So, "'I' didn't do it on purpose" usually means our conscious mind didn't intentionally plan or choose to do the problematic behavior. But the fact remains that we acted out the behavior. The conscious mind is clearly not in control. So, which level of our being is actually in charge of our behavior at the time, and does the fact that we don't consciously intend to do this erase or excuse the fact that we did it?

Here's a common example: Someone on a weight loss diet binge eats sweets while their conscious mind tells them not to do it. However, they still do it. Even worse, their conscious mind tries to bargain with their inner levels; they're just going to eat a few ___ (i.e., cookies, chips, pieces of candy), but somehow, they eat the whole bag. Even though they didn't consciously *mean* to eat the whole bag and sabotage their diet, that's still the result of their behavior.

Other popular, unhelpful conscious attitudes towards the unconscious mind and body include:

- "I don't believe in that."
- "It's not real (it's a dream, or something I imagined), so I can ignore it/it doesn't really bother me."
- "I can't (logically) explain why I feel this way (intuition), so the feeling/insight is not valid."
- "It's my religious or political philosophy that sex, meat, money, etc., are bad, so I should suppress my urges and go without them."

Your unconscious mind and body aren't going to like or cooperate with these attitudes.

If we are to have world peace, I believe we have to start with self-peace. To that end, I've developed Healing from the Body Level Up™ (HBLU™) methodology to:

1. Teach people how to understand and communicate clearly with all levels of their being, and
2. Heal any parts of them that aren't optimally serving the whole being. This allows us to align/coordinate all levels of our being so that our intentions match our behaviors and all parts of us work together to accomplish our life goals.

DIFFERENT LEVELS OF YOUR BEING CAN CARRY DAMAGE PATTERNS

Are you physically and emotionally healthy? Are you financially self-sufficient or even financially secure, or are you dependent or feel like there is never enough? Are you successful and happy in your career, or are you just working for the money? Do you feel loved and wanted, or do you feel disconnected and like you don't fit in? Are you able to give and receive love easily, or does your heart feel blocked or fearful? Do you feel your life has value to yourself, others, and the world, or do you feel lost or that life has no meaning? Are you having fun, are you happy, or do you feel bored, depressed, or anxious? Are you resilient, optimistic, and creative about navigating life problems? Are you continuing to grow and evolve, or do you feel stuck in your life?

If you aren't on track with your soul mission, or you feel uncomfortable or are not getting the desired results in some area of your life, then there must be some type of interference causing a misalignment at some level of your being.

The next question is, what type of interference can there be? I see three major categories of interference. The first two categories, Life Experience and Personality Structure, are internal to you. The last category, External Interference, is external to you.

INTERFERENCE FROM LIFE EXPERIENCE DAMAGE

The first major category is LIFE EXPERIENCE. In this category, I call whatever is interfering with you ***interference patterns*** or ***damage patterns***, and I use these terms interchangeably. These patterns are caused by events that occur in your life and imprint at three levels: in the conscious mind, the unconscious mind, and the body.

DAMAGE AT THE CONSCIOUS LEVEL

Examples of damage patterns at the conscious level include misinformation or lack of information and skills. Basic skills such as reading, writing, and math, balancing a checkbook, grocery shopping, cooking, and knowledge of proper nutrition are important for functioning as an independent adult, but many people lack these skills because of inadequate or incomplete education. Effective communication and relationship skills to connect with others and meet your and others' needs are essential, but often sadly lacking. Lack of healthy parenting skills causes a tremendous amount of damage to children, stunts their personal development, and then causes system-wide dysfunction even through future generations.

DAMAGE AT THE UNCONSCIOUS LEVEL

Examples of damage patterns at the unconscious level include limiting beliefs and bad habits that we pick up from our parents, friends, religion, and society.

A limiting belief (in NLP terminology), or sabotage program (in applied kinesiology terminology), or a reversal (in energy psychology terminology) is a belief that a person *feels* is true, but it's not objectively true. In fact, the belief is the reverse/opposite of the truth. People who are aware of their beliefs will even say, "I know better/I know this isn't true, but I feel this way."

Beliefs are stated in single sentences. Some common examples of limiting beliefs are, "I can't heal," "I'm unlovable," or "I'm unworthy (to live, of love, etc.)." Even if we "know better" and are consciously aware that the belief isn't rationally true, emotions still have a tendency to run our behavior, and we constantly struggle with it.

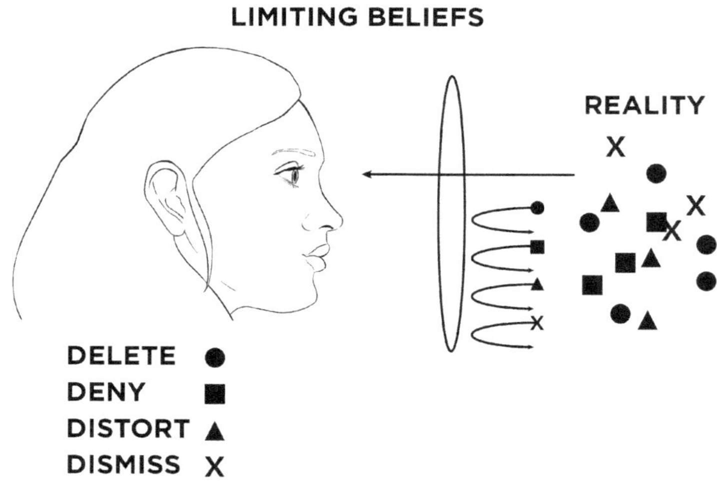

THE 4 D'S: DELETE, DENY, DISTORT, DISMISS

How do people manage to hold onto beliefs that aren't true? A belief forms a lens through which we filter all external information. Information that agrees with the belief gets through the filter, and we see it as validation, proof, or support for that belief. In other words, we see what we believe. On the other hand, information that disagrees with the belief gets *deleted, denied, distorted*, or *dismissed*.

Sometimes, when there's a tremendous amount of evidence that contradicts that belief, we give it up. This is called "live and learn." Live and learn can take a long time and may never happen. That's why it's much quicker and easier to use HBLU™ to clear limiting beliefs.

Pam and Gloria

Pam and Gloria went to a Jewish singles dance. Pam had a limiting belief: "I'm unattractive." After a while, Gloria noticed a man staring at Pam from across the room. The conversation went like this:

Gloria: "Hey Pam, that man has been staring at you for the last ten minutes."

Pam: "I don't see anyone staring at me." **(Delete)**

Gloria: "Are you kidding me? He's 6'4", wearing a navy-blue suit, powder blue shirt, and a red tie, standing next to the cookies."

Pam: "I see him, but he's not looking at me; he's looking at you." **(Deny)**

Gloria: "He sees us looking at him, and now he's walking this way and smiling at you."

Pam: "Okay, he's coming this way, but if he gets any closer or the lights get any brighter, he'll run the other way." **(Distort)**

Gloria: "I'm going to circulate. I'll see you later."

Pam: "Okay, he'll talk to me for ten minutes and decide he doesn't like me. Or, he'll ask for my phone number and then not call me. Or, we'll go out for coffee and after an hour, he'll decide he doesn't want to pursue this, so never mind." **(Dismiss)**

At the end of the evening, Gloria had contact information from three men, and Pam had none. Even worse, Pam said, "I told you so; there are no men who would be interested in me at these events." Gloria decided never to go to another singles event with Pam.

One of the most popular forms of distortion is, "That's the exception."

Abigail

When my client, Abigail, was 13 years old, she had a conversation with her father as follows:

Father: "Abigail, I want you to hide your intelligence around men because it will frighten them off."

Abigail: "But Daddy, you married Mom, a really intelligent woman."

Father: "Yes, but I'm the exception."

Abigail: "But Daddy, if there's one like you in this world, there are more like you in this world. And besides, how could I possibly respect a man who likes me because I'm stupid?"

Father (astonished): "Well, honey, I guess you're right."

WHAT CAUSES LIMITING BELIEFS?

1. A major cause of limiting beliefs is trauma. I describe trauma-derived limiting beliefs in detail in this book.

What ***other causes of limiting beliefs*** are there besides trauma?

2. Limiting beliefs can be caused by baby logic, when a child tries to explain something he observes but doesn't understand.

A 50-plus-year-old real estate agent, Jane, came to me because she felt depressed. The cause of this feeling was a limiting belief of, "I'm not important." In reality, she was happily married for 25 years, and at least one colleague from work liked her enough to refer her to me for treatment. Obviously, many people thought she was important.

Muscle testing revealed that this belief began at age five. (Muscle testing is described later in this chapter and in Chapter 8, Protocols.)

Sally had a speech impediment, and her parents wanted her to clear it up before she went to kindergarten so the other children wouldn't tease her. They decided to take her for speech therapy, which in those days was only offered at the university, an hour's drive from their home. Sally overheard her parents complain constantly about the commute. She also noticed her older sister never needed speech therapy and was perfect. Somehow, she put these facts together into the belief that she wasn't important.

As we looked into the five-year-old scene, we determined that Sally actually succeeded in clearing up the speech impediment before going to kindergarten. She was also certain that even if her parents had been forewarned about the logistical problems, they would've taken her for speech therapy anyway.

I said to adult Sally, "You're an adult now. Why would adults do something so admittedly difficult, arduous, and annoying?"

She immediately responded, "When it's important to them," and the limiting belief cleared.

3. Limiting beliefs can be learned by imitating parents or other family members.

One of the family jokes in Jim's family was, "You always spend more money than you make." Little Jim didn't know this was a joke, so when he got his first job and started running up credit card debt, he wasn't overly concerned. Sadly, Jim had to declare personal bankruptcy, an example of how a limiting belief can set someone up for trauma.

4. Some limiting beliefs are generalizations drawn from limited personal experience.

Priscilla had a limiting belief that "you can't lose weight without being hungry." It made perfectly logical sense to her that if the body is losing weight, it warns you by making you hungry. She was mystified that other people at Weight Watchers never complained about this. As she lost weight, her body was under constant stress, and if she ate too little in a day, she woke up hungry at 3:00 a.m. and was unable to sleep until she ate something.

One day, Priscilla heard someone talk about how they ate because they enjoyed it and because they craved sweets. She realized she never ate unless she was hungry. She didn't enjoy eating; it was a nuisance that interrupted work. *Maybe you can lose weight without being hungry*, she thought. A Weight Watchers facilitator confirmed this by suggesting she eat more protein and fewer carbohydrates.

Priscilla cleared the limiting belief with Unwinding Frontal/Occipital (U/FO Holding), ate a higher protein diet, and lost the weight she wanted to lose. Clearing the limiting belief opened the door to healing residual hunger and metabolic problems, and to treating her tendencies toward anorexia.

DAMAGE AT THE BODY LEVEL

To live a full life, it's important to have a fully functioning body. Damage patterns at the body level interfere with people achieving their goals by causing physical and emotional limitations. Examples of body-level damage include physical injuries, illnesses, and emotional traumas. In this book, I share many examples of treating trauma that causes physical symptoms.

If physical symptoms remain after releasing the trauma that caused them, I refer people for treatments that involve direct physical interventions. For example, after clearing physical injury trauma that caused joint damage to knees or hips, the individual may need joint replacement surgery to recover function. I found that if we clear the trauma associated with that part of the body, people recover more quickly and more fully than doctors typically expect for that type of treatment.

Body level damage also includes genetic deficits that can cause mental illness, learning difficulties (ADD/ADHD), and physical problems such as heart disease, hypothyroidism, Type 2 diabetes, cancer, and more. For genetic problems, I refer people for physical interventions including Western medical treatment (allopathic medicine), nutrition, homeopathy, chiropractic, acupuncture, and physical therapy, to name a few.

INTERFERENCE FROM PERSONALITY STRUCTURE

DAMAGE

The second major category of interference is PERSONALITY STRUCTURE. This is your ego structure or operating system (like a computer operating system). The personality structure sets your sense of self and your worldview. It's the filter through which you process all incoming and outgoing information.

There are many models of personality structure. I use the Enneagram model because I find it very useful. This model describes the nine different personality types and their areas of excellence. It also describes wounds of personality that cause compulsive behaviors and a distorted sense of identity and worldview that act like bugs in your operating system, and interfere with large areas of your life.

INTERFERENCE FROM EXTERNAL SOURCES

New Age ideas to the contrary, I don't believe we create or control *everything* that happens to us in the universe. Thus, the third major category is EXTERNAL INTERFERENCE. Examples of external factors that interfere with us are natural disasters, nasty people with *free will*, and supernatural phenomena. Even though these interferences are not about or from us, they still interfere with our lives.

HOW DO DAMAGE PATTERNS INTERFERE WITH US?

Damage patterns cause negative emotions. Emotions are energetic sensations felt in the body. That's why they are called *feelings*. Emotions have more energy than thoughts and therefore influence or run behavior. This explains the common phenomenon of "I know I shouldn't be doing X" while we're doing X.

Again, the conscious mind isn't in charge. Thus, damage patterns adversely influence our perceptions, reactions, and behavior in such a way as to make it difficult to achieve our goals. So, the most important issue here is to identify the type of interference, locate the negative emotions in the body, and use an effective technique or tool to clear out the pattern.

ADOPT ATTITUDE, AWWWWW, NEEDS HEALING

Information from the unconscious, body, and soul levels may be new to you consciously. You may be surprised at what's coming up, and might even experience the discovery of a damage pattern as painful. No one really *likes* to discover limitations. You may need to take 10-60 seconds to react and wince, but as soon as possible, move into an attitude of at least neutral acceptance if not downright compassion.

In a compassionate voice, say to yourself or out loud, like you would to an injured child: "Awwwww, needs healing." You don't need to love your damage, but you do need to accept that it *exists* before you can address it enough to focus on and heal it. Self-acceptance is easier said than done, but do your best to hold the attitude. As its own topic, self-acceptance is so important that you may even want to use it as a goal.

STARTING THE WORK

We start the work by consciously establishing clear communication with our unconscious minds, bodies, and souls. The first thing you need to do is **notice** when something isn't working properly for you. It's important to evaluate behaviors, beliefs, attitudes, emotional reactions, and end results according to whether or not they really work **for** you in the service of your highest good and purpose.

I suggest you focus less on whether something is true or not, and more on whether something is useful or not.

For example, when I moved to Washington, D.C., somebody told me it would be difficult for me to find a boyfriend because the ratio of women to men was 5:1. That might be statistically true, but not useful. I decided to believe I could always find someone right for me if I was open to all possibilities. In fact, I always had male company whenever I wanted it.

So, if you notice what you're doing or experiencing isn't working for you, check your beliefs, emotional reactions, and behaviors, and **ask questions** about them.

The first place to question is your unconscious mind. Remember, the unconscious mind doesn't use rational arithmetic or logic. It uses metaphorical, poetic logic. It's the land of dreams. Therefore, it's important to understand the communication style of the unconscious mind and recognize consciously when and how it's communicating.

The first step is to go inside yourself and ask the part of you that's doing (or not doing) the problematic behavior an open-ended question: "What are you feeling, what are you doing, what are you trying to tell me?" Send the question echoing throughout your whole body, top to bottom, front to back, and wait for a response. I call this an emotional CT scan. The response will come quickly and take the following forms:

1. Visual: a picture, a memory, a dream you can see.
2. Auditory: a thought in words, a piece of music, a tone of voice.
3. Kinesthetic: a physical or emotional sensation felt in the body. (Sometimes there's a taste or smell response.)

It's easy to interpret an auditory response in words. You will have to dialogue more with pictures or feelings to better understand what they're telling you.

There's a layer of information stored in the body that's difficult to access mentally. We get this information by using an applied kinesiology technique called muscle testing. Muscle testing is based on the same principle as lie detector testing; the body registers true or false answers to questions. We can get this same information without the expensive equipment by testing the difference in muscle strength on true and false statements.

We usually perform muscle testing by asking you to hold your arms out in front of you while the facilitator presses on them after asking a question. You can also self-test by using your fingers. Muscle testing allows us to get information from the unconscious mind, body, and soul, just by specifying which level you're asking the question of. For example:

- "From the body level, do you have any physical injury trauma in this muscle?"
- "From your deepest wisdom, is this the best plan of action in this situation?"

- "From your deepest wisdom, do we understand accurately this message from your unconscious mind?"

When I ask colleagues or new clients if they're familiar with muscle testing, they often say, "I'm familiar with it, but it doesn't work for me," "I don't trust my answers," or "I'm not confident I'm doing it right." I found muscle testing is always accurate, but you have to know how to interpret the signals you're getting. There are at least ten different patterns that cause unexpected or deceptive signals on muscle testing, and the first three days of my HBLU™ Module 1 training are devoted to learning to muscle test anyone accurately.

In the Protocols section of this book, for healing professionals who have some experience with muscle testing, I included instructions for muscle testing, a description of some common issues that cause confusion or inaccuracy, and a protocol for treating the most common blocks. I also included instructions for self-muscle testing.

Later, you'll learn two Do-It-Yourself Protocols for Treating Trauma. The Simple 4-Step Trauma Clearing Protocol for clearing trauma ***does not require muscle testing to be successful***. The Slightly More Sophisticated Trauma Clearing Protocol instructs people who know how to use muscle testing to use it to check that all aspects of the trauma have been completely cleared.

One of the features that makes HBLU™ so novel is that once you've established communication with all levels, **your deepest wisdom dictates *all* the goals, directions, and healing steps** we take during a session. Your deepest wisdom tells us what's interfering with you, where it's located in your body, and which interventions you want to use to clear it. The only trick is knowing the right questions to ask. What your therapist brings to the work is knowledge of the structure of the damage patterns, the quickest approach to healing them completely, and a menu of interventions that work efficiently and at all four levels.

This work is basically a two-step process:

1. Interview all the levels to find, name, and locate the damage pattern.

2. Use a technique to move negative energy and clear the damage pattern.

IN SUMMARY

I believe that the effectiveness of HBLU™ is due to four factors.

The process of asking your deepest wisdom to identify the priority goal and the priority interference pattern, having you explain the pattern consciously, and finally locating the negative energy or feelings in your body, allows all four levels to focus on and clear the problem simultaneously. I call this *aligning the levels.*

The first factor is connecting with your deepest wisdom to lead the healing.

The second factor is a comprehensive menu of damage patterns and knowledge of their structures.

The third factor is a comprehensive menu of rapid, effective techniques.

The fourth factor is specificity. By choosing the priority interference pattern from menu A and matching the appropriate intervention from menu B, each session is tailored to the individual.

The rest of this book is focused specifically on healing trauma, the most common pattern causing unconscious self-sabotage and suffering. In these pages, you will learn about the many types of trauma we all experience in our lives. You will learn a simple, easy-to-use protocol for releasing trauma from mind and body that combines knowledge of the structure of trauma with the Natural Bio-Destressing technique. It's my hope that empowering you with these resources will allow you to more easily create the life you want.

CHAPTER 1

THE REACTION IS THE PROBLEM

The **fight/flight/freeze reflex** is an automatic physical reaction to **perceived threat or danger**. This survival instinct exists in all animals and helps them to survive by preparing the body to fight off the threat, flee from the threat, or freeze to hide from the threat. So, the purpose of this reflex is to *save your life*.

The downside of this reflex is that it causes phobic reactions. A phobic reaction is a conditioned response of the fight/flight/freeze reflex that starts when a person experiences a traumatic shock (physical or emotional). At the time the fight/flight/freeze reflex fired off, anything that was in the environment could get associated with that memory. Later, these associations can trigger this original reflex reaction (like a body flashback), resulting in a phobic reaction, even when nothing dangerous or upsetting is happening (see Chapter 6 for an in-depth explanation of the neurobiology of trauma). Depending on the circumstances, the shock may imprint as a phobia, or in more severe cases, a trauma.

Survival is a good thing. The problem is that the ***reaction lasts long after the danger is over.***

In this chapter I describe the basic structure of phobias. In the next chapter I describe the basic structure of trauma.

THE BASIC STRUCTURE OF PHOBIAS

Many people think of phobias as a fear of flying, heights, or public speaking. But really, you can have a phobia of just about anything, even a phobia about being yourself.

What is a phobia? A phobia is an exaggerated, irrational emotional and physical reaction that's out of proportion with what's happening in reality. People with phobias find they can't mentally control or permanently talk themselves out of this reaction. Phobias range in severity from mild (a person may not even realize their anxiety is phobic) to severe (enough to send them into a panic or freeze them up completely). I usually ask people to rate their phobic response on the following scale of 1-10+:

DISCOMFORT SCALE

10+–I am numb, frozen; I feel nothing.

10–Panic. The discomfort is the worst it can possibly be. I can't tolerate it.

9–Discomfort is very close to intolerable.

8–Fear is very severe.

7–Fear is severe.

6–Fear is very uncomfortable.

5–Fear is uncomfortable, but I can tolerate it.

4–Fear is noticeable and bothersome, but I can deal with it.

3–I feel a slight degree of fear, but I'm totally in control.

2–I'm rather calm, quite relaxed, with no fear.

1–I am perfectly calm and totally relaxed.

PHOBIAS COME IN TWO FLAVORS: FEAR AND SHAME.

Fear phobias imply a life-threatening outcome and end in some form of death, eternal torment, or rejection. For example:

- "I'm afraid to speak in front of a large group of people I don't know because they will disagree with what I'm saying and kill me."
- "I'm afraid to feel angry because I will kill someone." Sometimes, people also add "and be sent to Hell" or "sent to outer darkness," a place worse than Hell.

Shame phobias involve character assassination, i.e., *there's something fundamentally wrong with me that I'm ashamed to admit.* For example:

- "I'm ashamed to speak in front of a large group of people I don't know because I'll forget what I'm saying and prove I'm a stupid idiot."
- "I'm ashamed to feel angry because it means I'm evil."

A ***shame and fear hybrid phobia*** example is:

"I'm ashamed and afraid to speak in front of a large group of people I don't know because I'll forget what I'm saying, look foolish/stupid, and be rejected."

A person can have more than one phobia on the same subject. In the case of fear of driving over bridges, I often see, "I'm afraid to drive over a bridge because it will collapse under me and I will die," and "I'm afraid to drive over a bridge because I will drive off the edge to my death."

In order to clear a phobia, it's necessary to use accurate wording. Phobias are extreme, black-and-white statements of the very worst things your unconscious mind and body imagined at the time of the initial shock. There are no maybes, woulds, coulds, or mights. Phobias are statements of certainty. If you don't name the most extreme version your unconscious mind and body imagined (imagination is a two-edged sword), you can't clear the complete phobia. So, in order to lighten up this process, I say, "We're going to play a television game show called Name That Phobia."

I remind my clients not to give me any limp wording; phobias are very highly charged.

Note: There is no such thing as a fear of the unknown. That is a strategy to consciously avoid where the unconscious mind went because it's too painful/scary. Remember, the unconscious mind knows what it imagined, and will tell us exactly what the phobia is so we can clear it.

HOW ARE PHOBIAS STRUCTURED?

Phobias commonly come as a two-part structure.

I. The **initial shock** is the reaction you experienced while in the phobic life situation. We clear this while you i*magine being in the moment* when the phobic reaction occurred. For example, with public speaking, imagine being on stage.

II. **Anticipatory phobias** are the dread that something bad will happen again in the future. We clear this using either the best or most highly charged example of experiencing the anticipatory phobia in the past. **Or**, we use the imaginary worst-case scenario of the future. For example, with public speaking, focus on the fear you felt when asked to give a speech, or the fear you feel backstage before getting in front of the audience.

HOW DO WE CLEAR PHOBIAS?

Conscious mind etiquette. The conscious mind is the land of rational, concrete, linear **logic**. It doesn't have feelings. The conscious mind can't release a phobia by arguing with it, denying it, criticizing it, or trying to talk or shame you out of it. The conscious mind's job is to find the area of the body where the phobia is located, interview it with compassion to map its story, and apply a technique to release the phobia (usually an energy psychology technique such as Natural Bio-Destressing).

NAME THAT PHOBIA

It's crucial to name the phobia precisely. Then we determine which example of the reaction is the best one to use. It's usually the most charged example—either the worst example or a recent one—that makes it easy to recall the feeling.

Note: When you clear the most emotionally charged example, it clears all the other repetitions of the pattern through all time (forward and backward).

Then, we concentrate on the feeling that memory evokes and use a technique—typically an energy psychology technique like NBD. These techniques activate the calming reflex and clear the phobia by neutralizing the fight/flight/freeze reaction and deactivating any triggering stimuli.

When a person has cleared the phobia, he's now normally cautious, as opposed to phobic. So, if you have a fear of snakes, you'll no longer react to a picture in a book, or to seeing them in a zoo. This doesn't mean you'll go handle them untrained. Remember, *you don't have to be frightened to be cautious.*

CHAPTER 2

THE BASIC STRUCTURE OF LOSS AND VIOLENCE TRAUMA IMPRINTS

When I first started practicing mind-body healing as a Neuro-Linguistic Programming (NLP) practitioner, I worked with many clients who presented with a diverse set of physical or emotional problems. Despite the variety of symptoms, I was fascinated to discover a large proportion of these problems were caused or exacerbated by trauma, primarily loss and violence. Some of the diverse manifestations of these trauma imprints included physical illnesses or symptoms such as immune system deficits (repeated infections, cancer, allergies, asthma), body pain (headaches, residual pain, or weakness from physical injuries), cardiovascular irregularities (heart palpitations), neuroendocrine irregularities (infertility), and sleep and energy level deficits.

Representative emotional problems included an inability to progress toward life goals (feeling "stuck"), such as obtaining a desired job or mate. I initially assumed the "frozen" quality of the problem was phobic in nature and would resolve after a simple phobia cure treatment. I soon discovered that loss and violence trauma imprints have additional components that require healing in order to obtain complete and lasting results. I decided to study and characterize the core structure of loss and violence trauma imprints to develop a thorough, successful, and rapid treatment protocol.

The trauma patterns and treatment protocols described here are the result of an in-depth study of more than 80 clients I treated over a period of ten years, and I first published the results in 1994 (1). I was intrigued to discover that all loss traumas have common core structures, and all violence traumas have common core structures. I also found that although the two patterns are quite similar, there are certain unique characteristics that distinguish a loss from a violence imprint. In this chapter, I share original and updated findings with additional case examples to illustrate some of the points more in depth.

HOW DOES TRAUMA OCCUR?

Trauma imprints occur in individuals' minds and bodies at the moment they first feel shocked, surprised, and/or frightened during a traumatic experience that triggers the fight/flight/freeze reflex. This imprint is phobic in nature, i.e., instantaneous and irrational at the moment of the initial shock. The imprint remains frozen in the body, and environmental cues can trigger flashbacks of the event unless the trauma imprint is specifically released by interventions like the Natural Bio-Destressing technique (described in Chapter 8) that clear phobic reactions directly from the body.

The major characteristic of a trauma imprint includes a sense of being frozen, stuck, unable to breathe, unable to change, and unable to access age-appropriate resources in specific situations. Additional diagnostic indicators include unwarranted, irrational, or exaggerated emotional reactions (responses that people know are inappropriate but are unable to suppress or control consciously), and repeating nightmares.

Trauma imprints are more complicated than simple phobias because they're layered. In addition to fear, there are the intense negative emotions of anger, sadness, hurt, and guilt or shame. At the same time, people make irrational decisions about themselves, the situation, and the world in general. These decisions can undermine their self-worth and confidence.

In my original study, I examined the structure of two major categories of trauma imprints: loss and violence. Experiences that predictably cause loss trauma imprints include unexpected loss of a family member, spouse, or friend through death or divorce, actual or apparent abandonment or betrayal, a sudden health crisis resulting in loss of function, and loss of a job. Experiences that predictably cause violence trauma imprints include direct or witnessed verbal, physical, or sexual attacks on individuals or their property. Sometimes a traumatic experience will cause an individual's personality to fragment into conflicting parts, and sometimes the damaged parts are suppressed.

In Neuro-Linguistic Programming, we believe all parts of you at all levels, including your conscious mind, unconscious mind, body, and soul, wish to preserve your health and well-being and are working, or trying to work, in your best interest. If your behavior and symptoms seem to be sabotaging you, we assume there are parts of you that need healing. Interestingly, when I find a part of a client who will not admit to having a positive intention and who can't be talked into updating their behavior to be more effective at their job, I know the client has experienced trauma.

Sometimes trauma incidents are so terrible that people's unconscious minds protect their conscious minds by entirely suppressing the memory of the event. In these cases, clients may suspect something bad has happened to them because they have repeated bad dreams or small flashes of memory, someone else tells them about the event, or they're aware their behavior and emotional reactions are different from those of others in similar situations.

It requires a lot of energy to consciously or unconsciously suppress and compensate for trauma reactions with all the negative emotions and limiting beliefs. This energy drain makes it difficult for people to be completely successful, to fully enjoy their life in the present, and to easily progress into the future. Like a dormant volcano, the whole experience can erupt at any time, causing anxiety and pain. If the trauma occurred early in life, it can freeze people's emotional development and block their ability to develop into powerful, resourceful, successful, productive, and complete adults.

From my specialization in phobias and in health problems, I found that many of my clients carried loss and violence imprints, even though they were not initially aware that this was the cause of their presenting problems. Two clients presented with seemingly simple phobias (fear of heights and claustrophobia in subways), which were in fact related to the loss of their fathers at age two to three years and at age eleven months, respectively. Several clients manifested compulsive/addictive behaviors such as workaholism, food addiction (binge-eating), and relationship addictions or dysfunctions stemming from loss or violence traumas.

Disease symptoms that disappeared following trauma intervention included side effects from cancer treatment, physical injury symptoms caused by acute episodes of multiple sclerosis, chronic fatigue syndrome, recurring viral upper respiratory infections, musculoskeletal pain, learning disabilities, interstitial cystitis, intestinal problems, headaches, and high blood pressure. In addition, 50-70% of allergies could be traced to an initial traumatic experience that needed to be cleared before the immune response could be permanently corrected (2).

If trauma imprints are so damaging to people, why do we have the neuroendocrine hardwiring for this physical reflex? A possible answer to this question came to me as I listened to a friend describe a motorcycle accident. Although he was badly injured, he felt no pain and was able to function well enough to get himself to a hospital. People who lose loved ones often make the funeral arrangements in a numb state that enables them to function. Clearly, this reflex is a survival mechanism that allows people to function without being overwhelmed by pain for 24-48 hours after an injury. (For more details, see Chapter 6.)

Interestingly, the fight/flight/freeze reflex is triggered by emotional trauma to the same degree as physical trauma. After wondering about this for years, I realized that the unconscious mind or body cannot distinguish physical from emotional pain since emotions are feelings felt in the body. Even the conscious mind has trouble distinguishing whether certain sensations are due to physical vs. emotional causes. It's common for people to confuse nausea or diarrhea caused by anxiety with symptoms caused by food poisoning or an intestinal virus. It's common for people to confuse the symptoms of a panic attack with those of a heart attack.

Regardless of what caused the trauma, the imprint remains frozen in the body until the person uses appropriate techniques for clearing trauma from the body. Because trauma was the predominant cause of my clients' physical, behavioral, and emotional symptoms, I decided to study trauma in depth. Through repeated testing and experience, I was able to map the core structure of loss and violence imprints in the conscious mind, unconscious mind, and body, and devise a treatment protocol for clearing the entire pattern.

The basic structure of loss and violence traumas is listed in outline form in the next two pages. An in-depth explanation of the structure follows. All the elements outlined in the core structure are common to every one of the clients studied. The exact wording of some of the core beliefs varies with the individual, but the meaning is the same. Additional beliefs not listed in the outline, underlying causes, and some of the behavioral manifestations associated with the imprint are unique to that individual in that situation.

The Do-It-Yourself Protocol for Treating Trauma in Chapter 8 gives instructions on how to use the trauma outlines in combination with NBD to clear trauma.

BASIC OUTLINE OF LOSS TRAUMA IMPRINTS

How many things did you lose or feel you lost in that trauma?
List all the losses and ask if they can all be cleared together.

I. NEGATIVE EMOTIONS
   A. Shock/Fear
   B. Anger/Rage
   C. Sadness/Sorrow
   D. Hurt/Pain

II. LIMITING (CORE) BELIEFS
   A. Responsibility (guilt/shame/blame)
      1. It's my fault because _________
      2. It's other people's fault because _________
      3. Disconnection from God. It's God's fault because _________ (How could God let this happen? There is no God.)
   B. Who will take care of me?
   C. People leave me. I can't trust them
   D. I am powerless or helpless/I have no control
   E. I am bad/unlovable/unwanted/undeserving/unworthy

III. FEELING OF EMPTINESS (Loss or Grief)

IV. OPTIONAL
   A. Bitterness/hate/disappointment/loneliness/other negative emotions
   B. Other limiting beliefs
   C. Irrational thoughts
   D. Parts that feel that I'm already dead
   E. Limiting decisions: I decided to do _________ because of this trauma
   F. Limiting identities: I am _________ (something negative)
   G. External messages: i.e., someone else saying it's your fault because, or other messages
   H. Do you need to do amend-making with or forgive yourself, others, or God?
   I. Root cause: The setup–was there an earlier trauma, grudge, or underlying belief that predisposed you or set you up to incur this trauma?

V. ANTICIPATORY PHOBIAS

VI. Do I need to treat again to clear all the places in mind, body, and life where this imprint has been stored?

BASIC OUTLINE OF VIOLENCE TRAUMA IMPRINTS

Who did you feel perpetrated violence and what did they do that was violent?

Note: Sexual violence, past life, and genealogical/ancestral traumas should only be treated by a professional.

I. NEGATIVE EMOTIONS

A. Shock/Fear

B. Anger/Rage

C. Sadness/Sorrow

D. Hurt/Pain

II. LIMITING (CORE) BELIEFS

A. Responsibility (guilt/shame/blame)

1. It's my fault because __________.

2. It's other people's fault because __________.

3. Disconnection from God. It's God's fault because __________. (How could God let this happen? There is no God.)

B. Safety

1. My boundaries have been violated or breached.
2. I don't feel safe/I feel vulnerable.
3. I am a victim/I am a target.
4. People/men/women are dangerous and/or crazy.
5. I don't trust anyone.
6. I can't receive from anyone.

C. Power and control issues

1. I am powerless/helpless. I have no control.
2. Power is bad.
3. I am afraid of power (mine and or other people's).

D. I am bad/unlovable/unwanted/undeserving/unworthy.

III. FEELING OF POLLUTION

IV. OPTIONAL

A. Bitterness/hate/disappointment/loneliness/other negative emotions.

B. Other limiting beliefs.

C. Irrational thoughts.

D. Parts that feel that I'm already dead.

E. Limiting decisions: I decided to do __________ because of this trauma.

F. Limiting identities: I am __________ (something negative).

G. External messages: i.e., someone else saying it's your fault because, or other messages.

H. Do you need to do amend making with or forgive yourself, others, or God?

I. Root Cause: The setup–was there an earlier trauma, grudge, or underlying beli ef that predisposed you or set you up to incur this trauma?

V. ANTICIPATORY PHOBIAS

VI. Do I need to treat again to clear all the places in mind, body, and life where this imprint has been stored?

IN-DEPTH EXPLANATION OF TRAUMA STRUCTURE

LOSS TRAUMA IMPRINT

I. NEGATIVE EMOTIONS

The initial shock always occurs the moment a person first knows that something is wrong. Usually, the person learns the bad news in a phone call, in a face-to-face meeting, or by first-hand experience (e.g., watching someone collapse and later die). In that instant, the body imprints a shock which is often characterized by an intense adrenaline rush of fear, a feeling of frozenness or numbness, and/or a sharp indrawn breath followed by an inability to breathe normally. Exclamations of "I don't believe it," or "It can't be true," are common. The entire pattern with all its layers imprints simultaneously with the initial feeling of A. Shock/Fear. In addition, the body imprints feelings of B. Anger/Rage, C. Sadness/Sorrow, and D. Hurt/Pain.

II. LIMITING (CORE) BELIEFS

A. Responsibility (guilt/shame/blame).

When individuals suffer a loss, they try to make sense of it or understand why it happened.

1. It's my fault _________.

People believe that somehow the loss is their fault, feel guilty or ashamed, and arrive at an irrational conclusion. The client whose father died when she was 11 months old concluded that he died because she was born, and somehow, a life was traded for a life. A client whose mother suffered an aneurysm felt that his mother left him because he made her angry. One client whose father left when she was two years old concluded that he left because she didn't behave. A client whose sister was murdered wished she could've died in her sister's place in order to spare her. Another client whose brother died felt that her mother secretly wished she (the client) had died instead.

2. It's other people's fault because ________.

They blame other people, usually the other parent or other family members, for the loss. "It's Mommy's fault (that Dad left us) because she was afraid to leave Grandma." "It's Grandma's fault (that Dad left us) because she was always telling Mommy what to do." "It's the doctor's fault because he didn't do his job right."

3. Disconnection from God. It's God's fault because ________.

The underlying presupposition is that God is a benevolent, all-powerful, parental figure who is in control of the universe and whose job it is to protect you and make things work out okay. When something traumatic happens, people feel betrayed, let down, and disconnected from this God. People describe this reaction in many ways, including:

"How could God let this happen?"

"It's not fair!"

"Why does this have to happen to me?"

"Fate is against me."

"I'm jinxed/cursed."

"I've lost my faith and can no longer pray."

In cases where the loss is purely accidental (e.g., a ruptured aneurysm, a traffic or sports accident, a weather-induced fatality), individuals blame God (fate, the universe) for the loss and lose their sense of spiritual connection to God. Even in cases where the loss was not accidental (e.g., divorce or loss of a romantic relationship), the client often feels "destined for bad luck."

Harold Kushner, in his book *When Bad Things Happen to Good People*, states that in order for there to be free will, God cannot control everything and thus is not all-powerful (3). Random tragedies ". . .do not reflect God's choices. They happen at random, and randomness is another name for chaos. And chaos is evil; not wrong, not malevolent, but evil nonetheless, because by causing tragedies at random, it prevents people from believing in God's goodness." (3). The tragedy here is that trauma cuts people off from their spiritual resources, regardless of their conscious mind's perspective and personal definition of God.

B. Who will take care of me?

People who experience a loss worry about who will be there to meet their (financial, emotional, physical, social, etc.) needs. This question is especially charged for people whose parents died when they were still minors. One supporting parent is dead or has left, so the other parent could also die or leave (anticipatory phobia). Children too young to support themselves financially (and in other ways, i.e., "Who will love me?"), feel their survival is at risk. This particular feeling triggered workaholic behavior in two clients. A third client alienated her teenage daughter by chastising the girl for taking business track instead of college prep courses in high school. Her constant refrain was, "Without a college education, who will take care of you?" This question is also especially charged for spouses who are aging and worry about who will take care of them as they age. One client decided to get a Ph.D. after her husband (who is still alive nearly 15 years later) had a near-fatal heart attack.

C. People/men/women leave me. I can't trust them.

This belief generalizes across many contexts. It manifests behaviorally as a fear of beginning friendships as well as behavior that causes the loss of friendships. People with this belief feel unable to share their feelings and are afraid to show their "real self" to anyone else.

D. I am powerless or helpless/I have no control.

This belief manifests itself as a feeling that the person is unable to prevent the loved one from leaving. One client expressed it as, "I can't hold on to people I love." In some cases, people feel unable to even influence improvements in a relationship, although they may be aware that their actions can make the situation worse.

E. I am bad/unlovable/unwanted/undeserving/unworthy.

This belief also comes in the form of, "I have no value." Behaviorally, these individuals wonder about and are suspicious of people who like them. They feel the attention they're getting is, at some level, undeserved and unwarranted. Often, they feel it's necessary to bribe people for their love, friendship, and attention by taking care of them, doing something for them, or by trying to make themselves into whatever they imagine the other person wants them to be. People often remain in or cling to emotionally empty or abusive relationships because they feel unworthy or undeserving of a good relationship or of getting their needs met.

The core issue in *job loss trauma* is the feeling that "My work has no value." Regardless of any facts about why they were laid off, including the elimination of their entire department or the bankruptcy of the whole company, these people still believe the job loss was their fault. Their resulting lack of confidence causes them to radiate uncertainty during job interviews. They're often willing to take a pay cut or a lower-level position in their next job.

The core issue in *adoption trauma* for the child who has been given up is the feeling that "I'm unwanted." Trauma being irrational, the fact that the adoptive parents went to the ends of the Earth (China) and paid lots of money to adopt this baby, thus proving how much they wanted this child, doesn't register. The fact that the adoptive parents were infertile and were so happy to find a child to complete them doesn't matter. Even if the child was adopted by another member of the family (usually aunts, uncles, or grandparents), they still feel unwanted. This feeling is exacerbated whenever an adoptive family member routinely mentions that this child was adopted during introductions (to people who don't need to know and don't really care). The underlying message to the adoptee is, "You don't belong."

This accounts for some adoptees' compulsion to find their birth mother and father. What they really want to know is, "Why did you give me away?" The adoptee seeks reassurance that they weren't given away because there was something wrong with them.

Often, birth parents feel guilty for giving away their baby. Regardless of the real circumstances at the time (i.e., the mother was too drug addicted, young, poor, in an abusive relationship, being punished by her family or religion to keep or take care of a baby), the mother—and even sometimes the biological father—feels that they were bad for giving the child away.

John was a big, strong six-plus-foot, 37-year-old man with severe Down Syndrome. He was given up for adoption at an early age, was a ward of the state, and lived in several foster homes over his lifetime. When he came to see me, he lived in a group home where he participated in running the household and was particularly fond of chopping wood.

John's caretaker, Sam, brought him to me because John frequently erupted into violent fits of uncontrollable rage or grief that could be a danger to himself and others. Sam thought these reactions were caused by loss trauma. When I expressed apprehension about treating John, Sam assured me he would assist in the therapy session and that John would be safe to treat.

John's last home had been with a family—a mother, a father, and their son. Two years previously, the father died, and the son went to college, leaving the mother to care for John by herself. She couldn't handle taking care of John alone, so she simply ran away. John was left alone in the apartment for three weeks before social services found him.

Our session took place just before Christmas. John was verbally incoherent, but Sam assured me he understood everything we said. Although Sam thought John functioned at a ten-year-old level, I believed it possible that his level of function was younger than that, and understood John must have been really frightened by this abandonment.

John muscle tested well, and his deepest wisdom answered muscle-testing questions accurately. I very gently asked John, "Can you draw a picture about why you feel sad and angry?" John drew a long red rectangle. When I asked him to tell me about the picture, he talked incoherently at length, and Sam said, "I think he's saying something about Santa Claus."

With John talking, Sam attempting to translate, and me checking the answers by muscle testing, we elicited Sam's story. The red rectangle was Santa Claus. Santa Claus thought John was bad and punished him by taking his mother away. John just wanted Santa Claus to bring his mother back to him for Christmas. We treated John for the complete loss trauma outline.

I finished by asking Sam, "Have they located John's mother?" He confirmed they had. We arranged for Sam to invite her for a visit on Christmas. John's emotional outbursts stopped after our session.

III. FEELING OF EMPTINESS

The two unique characteristics that distinguish a loss from a violence trauma imprint are Category IIB (Who will take care of me?) and Category III. This feeling is generally described as a loss or grief reaction, but it's only part of a whole loss trauma imprint. When individuals experience a loss, they miss the person who's gone. The sense of loss manifests itself as an empty or hollow feeling in the area of the stomach, or in the area of the heart or chest.

This pattern may manifest itself as a belief that "I will never find another _________ as good as the one I lost." It may trigger addictive behavior; several clients developed eating addictions to fill the empty feeling associated with loss or rejection. One client lost his first business and subsequently developed addictive eating habits with an accompanying weight problem. Prior to the loss, he had a whole feeling in his chest, which he associated with a sense of confidence. After the loss, he felt a hole the size of his fist in that area of his chest.

This sensation may also lead to a desire to die. A client whose parents divorced when she was five years old described it eloquently. "I have such a feeling of emptiness that I have no ambition or curiosity about the world. Life is not worth living. I want to die." Another client, whose sister was murdered, pictured herself as an empty and barren (lifeless) meteor crater.

IV. OPTIONAL

The category labeled Optional signifies aspects of a trauma that may be present for that particular individual in that particular context, but are not necessarily present in every trauma.

A. Bitterness / hate / disappointment / loneliness / other negative emotions.

B. Other limiting beliefs (a one-sentence structure that you believe is true but was not ever true).

C. Irrational thoughts (a one-sentence structure that, when you imprinted this belief, it was true in that one situation, but it's not true as a generality). A woman who had birth trauma and was pulled out of the womb with forceps imprinted the belief that "men are out to get me." It was literally true at the time, but she generalized it to all men and never married.

D. Parts that feel like I'm already dead.

E. Limiting decisions (I decided to do _________ because of this trauma).

F. Limiting identities [I am _________ (something negative)].

G. External messages (i.e., someone else saying it's your fault because, or other messages).

H. Do you need to do amend-making with or forgive yourself, others, or God? This often clears with the beliefs "It's my, other people's, or God's fault because." Any remaining issues can be treated with one of the techniques described in this book or by making an apology or taking another type of corrective action.

You will see examples of these items in the many case examples I describe throughout the book.

I. ROOT CAUSE: The setup.

This category is considered optional because not every trauma has a root cause, and if there is one, it is unique to the individual in that situation. Usually, if someone loses a relationship or job, we look for the underlying beliefs and attitudes that contributed adversely to the situation. I've treated several unmarried women in their forties for painful relationship breakups. These women all have a history of attracting or being attracted to emotionally or physically abusive men. Not surprisingly, all these women had fathers who emotionally or physically abused their mothers.

One of my clients lost three businesses in three years (damaging his partners financially in the process) and got a divorce. The root cause was his father's death. When we cleared this imprint, he started a new business, got a new girlfriend, and maintained these relationships for at least five years after I treated him.

V. ANTICIPATORY PHOBIA

The anticipatory phobia is common to many simple phobias as well as to trauma imprints. It's the fear that the traumatic event will happen again, and is characterized by a pervasive, underlying feeling of dread. The specific manifestation of an anticipatory phobia is unique to that individual in that situation, but there are common themes. People who've suffered a loss fear they will lose other people they love. Clients often fear that the pain of another loss would be too much for them to bear ("If one of my children died, it would kill me.").

An elementary school teacher told me of a student in her class whose parents recently divorced, with Dad leaving the house. The child became noticeably anxious at the end of each school day, fearing that Mom wouldn't be there either when he got home. Parents who experienced childhood loss often appear to be overprotective or over-controlling. The client whose mother died of an aneurysm when he was eight years old was afraid of losing his wife and child. While walking in a large field with his two-year-old son, the child let go of his hand and ran ahead of him. Even though the road was quite a distance away, and even though there was no traffic, my client vividly imagined his child being run over and experienced a full-body reaction of panic.

Another client who experienced a severe illness worried obsessively about the possibility of his wife and daughter becoming ill. Sometimes people actively "kill off" relationships or businesses because of the belief that "everything comes to an end" or "nothing lasts forever." Thus, they end the arrangement themselves instead of waiting interminably for the inevitable to happen.

I have treated many families where there has been a divorce. I found that children want parents who love each other and function as competent adults in life. This allows children to feel secure. When there is a divorce, the children experience a loss trauma, and in many cases, hope their parents will work through their problems and stay or get back together.

When a parent wants to find a new partner and move on after a divorce, the children (especially children still living at home) often react with hostility towards the new romantic interest. The children's reactions are caused by the anticipatory phobias that the new love interest will prevent their parents from reuniting, and that ***they will be replaced*** by the new partner. Children may even blame the new partner for destroying their parents' marriage and their family ("It's other people's fault because"), rather than putting the blame on their parents, where it really belongs. This is why it's so difficult for parents to get their children to accept the new partner. Hostility may diminish over time, but it doesn't completely abate unless the children (as well as the parents) are treated for the loss trauma.

VIOLENCE TRAUMA IMPRINT

I. NEGATIVE EMOTIONS

The initial shock in a violence trauma imprint occurs at the moment individuals realize they're in physical danger (real or perceived). This occurs at the moment of violent contact, either physical or verbal. As in the case of loss, the entire pattern with all of its layers imprints simultaneously with the initial feeling of A. Shock/Fear. In addition, the body imprints feelings of B. Anger/Rage, C. Sadness/Sorrow, and D. Hurt/Pain. In the case of physical violence, the feeling of Hurt/Pain may refer to emotional as well as physical pain. If the Shock/Fear is not cleared immediately, the person who felt attacked often experiences flashbacks of violence, which may later subside into repeated nightmares in which someone (a monster) is attacking them. Several clients also reported severe emotional reactions when they identified with dead animals they passed on the road.

II. LIMITING (CORE) BELIEFS

A. Responsibility (guilt/shame/blame).

This category imprints identically to that of a loss imprint. Recipients of violence try to rationalize the crime by assigning responsibility.

1. It's my fault because _________.

They believe that somehow the attack was their fault. Statements like, "I should have known better than to go out with him, dress like that, walk unescorted in this area, etc.," are common. One client (at age five) was tied to her bed in the middle of the night after she called her father for a drink of water. She believed it was her fault because she should have known better than to ask her father for a drink of water. One client's drunken father attempted to kill his wife by shooting at her. The client believed the incident was her fault because she couldn't find a baseball bat in time to stop him.

2. It's other people's fault because _________.

They blame other people (except the perpetrator) for the attack. In the case cited above, the client believed it was her mother's fault for allowing herself to be attacked by going downstairs to investigate the noise her father was making as he loaded and unloaded his gun. In cases where people are the direct recipients of violence from within the family, they're often angry with the other parent or relatives for not protecting them from the violent parent. If violence comes from outside the nuclear family, they're angry with their parents, their neighbors, the police, the government, etc. for not protecting them.

3. Disconnection from God. It's God's fault because _________.

"How could God let this happen? There is no God." Beliefs about God and fate are the same as in a loss trauma imprint, with the addition of, "God should have protected me."

In this category of responsibility associated with a violence trauma imprint, I rarely see a client blame the actual perpetrator until after limiting beliefs are cleared. Usually, the person makes excuses for the perpetrator. One client presented with allergies, which started immediately after she moved in with her boyfriend, who beat her twice a week. She told me he really loved her, but he just snapped sometimes, and she didn't want me to be mad at him. Other people use excuses such as, "He was drinking and always played with his gun when he got drunk," or "He was crazy and couldn't help himself." Often, the person believes that if they only understood why the perpetrator did it (always assuming there's a rational reason), then the whole feeling of upset around the incident would disappear, and everything would be okay.

Many people have difficulty with the concept that human beings are capable of evil behavior. According to Harold S. Kushner, if there is truly free will, then God doesn't control everything and isn't responsible for the behavioral choices of man. "But if man is truly free to choose, if he can show himself as being virtuous by freely choosing the good when the bad is equally possible, then he has to be free to choose the bad also." (3) "... Human beings are free to choose the direction their life will take. Granted, some children are born with physical or mental capacities that limit their freedom of choice. Granted further, that some parents mishandle their children badly, that accidental events–wars, illnesses–traumatize children so badly that they may not be able to do something they would otherwise be qualified for, and that some people are so addicted to habits that it is hard to speak of them as being free. But I will insist that every adult, no matter how unfortunate a childhood he had or how habit-ridden he may be, is free to make choices about his life. ...To say of any criminal that he did not choose to be bad but was a victim of his upbringing, is to make all morality, all discussion of right and wrong, impossible." (3).

None of my clients experienced violence in a situation (such as war) where the violence against them could be rationally justified or expected. The irrational conclusions explaining the attack didn't make my clients feel any better. It was violent behavior that induced a trauma imprint, and "understanding" did not clear the damage at the body level. Thus, clearing the negative emotions and limiting beliefs around the responsibility issues is not linked to finding a way to excuse the perpetrator or to justify what he did (a common misconception of the definition of forgiveness). Rather, we clear the negative emotional charge and limiting beliefs because it's bad for your health and well-being to carry around this kind of emotional distress. When we finish clearing this section of the imprint, my clients are able to say, "What the perpetrator did was wrong, and I am okay."

B. Safety.

1. My boundaries have been violated or breached.

2. I don't feel safe/I feel vulnerable.

3. I am a victim/I am a target.

There are two unique characteristics that distinguish a violence imprint from a loss trauma imprint. The first of these is lack of safety, identified by B.1, B.2, and B.3. People have a sense of body perimeter or personal space which forms an energetic boundary surrounding them, and assume they have a choice about whom they allow to be physically or emotionally close and in what manner. The second unique characteristic of a violence imprint is III. Feeling of Pollution, described below.

During a violence incident, the attacker violates that space, thereby shattering the boundary and the feeling of choice. The person who felt attacked is left feeling vulnerable, unsafe, and possibly a victim or a target. Thus, manifestations of "I am not safe" are uniquely diagnostic of violence.

After an episode of emotional violence, the recipient is reluctant (feels intimidated) to engage the perpetrator in conversation. Immediately after a physical violence episode, the recipient may feel afraid to leave their homes or to let anyone physically near them. Later, this part of the imprint can develop into compulsive behavior. One client checked the locks on the windows and doors of her home several times every night before she went to bed (even though she lives with her husband). In the most severe forms of violence with a sexual component, people may shrink from being touched in any way, by anyone in any context.

4. People/men/women hurt me and/or are dangerous and/or are crazy.

Although these beliefs are imprinted during a specific violence incident, people generalize these beliefs across many contexts. I commonly see people who have been physically or emotionally abused by a parent generalize that all people of that gender are dangerous. They remain unconsciously guarded and have difficulty creating romantic relationships or even friendships with people of that gender.

5. I don't trust anyone.

People who have experienced violence approach other people with an *a priori* attitude of distrust. They assume other people are untrustworthy until proven otherwise and wait expectantly for misbehavior to surface.

6. I can't receive from anyone.

People view gifts and acts of kindness with suspicion ("What does this person want from me?"). They find it difficult to ask for help and feel fearful of relying on anyone else for anything they deem important. These beliefs interfere with their ability to make friends, cooperate interdependently in groups, learn from supervisors or mentors, and have intimate relationships.

C. Power and control issues.

1. I am powerless/helpless. I have no control.

These beliefs manifest themselves as, "I am powerless to prevent (or cannot control) other people from attacking me or hurting me." Often, people become the target for bullies because they refuse to defend or even assert themselves, believing they're incapable of it or that by defending themselves, they'll only make matters worse. They are unaware that defending themselves often obtains respect from those around them and can actually limit or prevent an attack.

The situation can be complicated when the bullies are family members of the person. The individual feels conflict about visiting or maintaining a connection with the family. Often, their previous therapists recommend that they stay away from the abusers. The person often feels offended that the therapist is trying to isolate him from his family. At the rational level, it's a question of physical or emotional safety, but at the emotional level, the person feels the attachment ("Blood or a marriage bond is thicker than water."). To avoid this conflict, I recommend that my clients wait to visit their families until they can protect themselves appropriately.

We clear limiting beliefs in this category so the person can access their full adult power and acknowledge responsibility for their own safety. Then we discuss practical ways to visit safely, such as staying in a hotel close to the family home, having a car so the person can freely exit a problematic situation, or visiting the family only in public places.

One of my clients, whose father had seriously injured him as a child, went to visit the family. His father attempted to get his attention during a group discussion by kicking him in the leg. My client calmly told his father not to kick him. His father kicked him again. My client then told his father not to kick him using such a ferocious tone of voice that he attracted the attention of the whole family and froze his father mid-motion. His father did not kick him again for the rest of the visit or during subsequent visits that year.

During her childhood, another client's father regularly beat her mentally ill mother to the ground and occasionally hit the client. As an adult, the client visited her father once a year on a holiday. During her visit the previous year, her father slapped her across the face and demanded that she "come in the house right now." When I asked her why she didn't fend off the blow or grab his hand to stop him, she replied that she was afraid it would incite him to further violence. When I asked her why she visited him, she replied, "Because he wanted me to." After we worked on this issue, she called to inform him she wouldn't visit him that year because he had beaten her the previous year. He actually apologized (my client was shocked), and my client did not visit him that year.

2. Power is bad.

People who have experienced violence feel that power is bad and generalize this belief to all contexts by assuming anyone who acts powerfully in the world will automatically misuse it. After we clear this belief, we discuss the fact that power, like electricity, money, or knowledge, isn't inherently good or bad. The context in which these are used determines the value judgment.

3. I am afraid of power, mine or other people's.

People often feel afraid of hurting others if they truly accessed their power. During adolescence, a client attempted to murder her stepfather, who repeatedly molested her. She hit him in the back of the head with a large beer bottle, causing the bottle to shatter, and her stepfather to get angry and slap her. She felt so guilty about assaulting this man that she decided to give up all her power. She became meek and submissive and remained that way until she began therapy in her late thirties. Upon hearing this story, I asked her, "Did hitting your stepfather on the back of the head succeed in getting him to stop molesting you?" She remarked with surprise that, in fact, he had not molested her again. She was so quick to relinquish her power that she never acknowledged the benefit of her actions.

D. I am bad/unlovable/unwanted/undeserving/unworthy.

This belief manifests in similar ways to that of a loss trauma imprint.

III. FEELING OF POLLUTION

The second unique characteristic of a violence imprint is III. Feeling of Pollution. The recipient feels polluted, dirtied, tarnished, sullied, touched by evil, etc. In cases of sexual violence (which induces a more severe trauma imprint than in cases of non-sexual violence), the feeling of pollution can manifest as extreme shame. A desire to wash off the feeling of the attacker is common.

IV. OPTIONAL

Although A through H are discussed in the previous section for Loss Trauma, there are other types of root causes for violence trauma.

IV. I. ROOT CAUSE: The setup.

Sometimes, when a person experiences violence, there is no root cause. It was just a random act of violence or chaos. For clients who experience repeated episodes of violence, I often look for an initial violence trauma in their early childhood that would make them susceptible to accepting, attracting, or inciting violence from strangers, acquaintances, friends, or family members. This is consistent with the assumption that the unconscious mind causes a person to regenerate patterns from earlier in his life in cases where there are unresolved emotions or issues.

Sometimes the root cause is a limiting belief that renders one susceptible to violence. A client presented with a history of chronic vaginal infections. In our initial phone conversation, I asked her whether she had experienced rape or incest. She explained that she had been subjected to incest from the age of one and a half to 15 years of age, first by her grandfather, and later by her brother. During previous therapy, she cleared about half of the violence trauma imprint, but never cleared the initial shock or root cause. I thanked her body for keeping her attention on unfinished business and promised we would certainly address the remaining issues.

She made an appointment for several weeks later and did not experience any more infections (previously, she consistently experienced three to four infections in that time frame) from the time of the initial telephone call through the six months I followed her. My initial approach was to take her back in time to the first incest experience and clear the shock/fear. Afterwards, she said she remembered staying at her grandparents' house and feeling fear when her grandfather came to take her out of bed.

During the experience, however, she never cried out or screamed, even though her grandmother was somewhere in the house. When I asked her why she was silent even though she knew something was wrong, she replied, "It doesn't do any good to complain when bad things happen because no one will respond." I asked her to go back into the incest scene, scream, and find out what might happen. In the rerun of the scene, Grandmother responded to her scream, rescued her from Grandfather (divorced Grandfather), and my client was never molested by him again.

Clearly, the belief that it does no good to complain rendered her susceptible to mistreatment and was the root cause of repeated violence in her life. We traced this belief back in time three generations on her mother's side. At the unconscious level, my client had a "memory" of a time when her great-grandmother was ten years old. The girl's mother had just died, and the father of the family was so grief-stricken that he withdrew emotionally. The little girl was rebuffed when she tried to share her grief with her father, and furthermore was told by neighbors, "Don't bother your father now. Can't you see he's upset?" She concluded, "It doesn't do any good to complain when bad things happen because no one will respond." Furthermore, she passed this belief down through the generations.

V. ANTICIPATORY PHOBIA

The anticipatory phobia in a violence imprint is the fear that someone or something will hurt you again, and this next time will be so much worse than the first experience that *this time* you will not survive. Anticipatory phobias of violence are particularly problematic in romantic relationships. The ability to be intimate with someone is a very important quality in a nurturing relationship. The dictionary defines intimacy as the feeling or atmosphere of closeness and openness towards someone else, not necessarily involving sexuality. My definition of intimacy is the ability to share (i.e., communicate) your innermost thoughts and feelings with another person. This requires the ability to connect with your unconscious mind, body, and soul, and have the words to describe your inner experience. This is a real skill set that takes training and practice to develop.

Many people think of developing these skills as learning to be "vulnerable." However, the word vulnerable actually means you have some kind of weakness that leaves you *open to attack*. The very word implies that you have to develop enough trust in someone to open yourself to them and hope they won't attack you. The assumption that loving relationships contain the potential for violence comes from traumatic experiences of violence. No wonder people are afraid to be vulnerable in a relationship. After I treat people for trauma, they no longer fear sharing their truth and describe this set of relationship skills as the ability to be emotionally available, genuine, authentic, honest, present, or open. The best definition I've heard from a member of our HBLU™ family is to be *emotionally accessible*!

SOME UNEXPECTED WAYS PEOPLE EXPERIENCE VIOLENCE TRAUMA

In situations where there is a physical assault, it is obvious who is the perpetrator of violence and who is the recipient of violence. But sometimes things such as germs causing a bad infection, or natural disasters, or healthcare professionals who are trying to help you, can be assigned as perpetrators of violence. Sometimes, a person who engages in self-destructive behavior assigns themselves as perpetrators of violence *against themselves.*

Both perpetrators and recipients of violence are traumatized.

Both men and women perpetrate violence.

Tom and Tanya

Tom spent time studying and just hanging out with Tanya, a college classmate. Over spring break, they realized they missed each other and texted every day. Curious, the next time they met, Tom kissed her. Although kissing was nice, Tom didn't feel a spark. He regretfully told her that he didn't have romantic feelings for her.

Tanya started crying and screamed at him for leading her on. Tom imprinted as a perpetrator of violence trauma. He needed to treat his feelings of shame for hurting her and the belief, "It's my fault because I led her on." Tom decided to give Tanya a couple of days to calm down and then talk with her about continuing the friendship they did have.

Jason

During an argument with his wife, Jason lost his temper and pushed her into the garage door. Neighbors called the police. He was convicted of assault, and his wife divorced him. Jason came to see me because he wanted to heal his violence patterns. We treated the garage door scene as a perpetrator of violence trauma, and found that the root cause was physical abuse by his father that imprinted in Jason's unconscious mind as normal relationship behavior.

Military Personnel

I have treated many military personnel for war trauma. Anyone who saw active duty in a war zone—even if they were firing weapons from a distance and never saw the people they were fighting, and even if they believed in the value of the cause they were fighting for—muscle tested positive for the belief, "I am a murderer." Military personnel who didn't see active combat did not have this belief.

Hilda and Frank

Hilda was married to Frank, an alcoholic. Thinking she was being a good wife, Hilda stayed up late drinking with him to keep him company. Eventually, Hilda's body couldn't take it anymore, and she stopped drinking with him. A few weeks later, Frank fell instantly in love with and started dating a young grocery store cashier. Incredulous, Hilda insisted they go for couples counseling. After writing contract after contract promising he would stop, and immediately taking the cashier out again, the therapist pointed out that there was nothing she could do if Frank didn't keep his word. Frank confirmed, "I'm going to do whatever I want, and you can't stop me."

At home that evening, five-foot-two-tall Hilda started screaming at six-foot-four-tall Frank and slapped him hard in the face. Frank pushed her hard into the bookcase. Hilda slapped him again. Frank called 911, had Hilda arrested (in handcuffs) for domestic violence, filed a restraining order against her, and then demanded she come home with him.

The next day, she came to see me. She was shocked and ashamed that she had lost control of herself and perpetrated violence. Although I commiserated with the part of her that felt he deserved a beating, I also agreed with her conscience that violence isn't the answer. We treated Hilda for the perpetrator of violence trauma. Then I recommended she move out of their home that afternoon (which she did) and divorce him as soon as possible (which she also did).

Abigail

Abigail was an overweight, middle-aged woman who hadn't been on a date in years. She came for help to lose weight and find love. We discovered that the priority interference on her goal was a perpetrator of violence trauma at age three. Abigail was carrying her one-year-old brother down the steps by herself when she fell on the last step and dropped her brother.

Hearing the baby scream, her mother came running and (external message) must have said something like, "What are you trying to do? Kill your baby brother?" Abigail concluded, "It's my fault that I tried to kill my baby brother because I'm jealous of him." She also made a limiting decision that, "I'm dangerous to men, so I have to protect them by keeping them away from me." She did this by gaining weight to make herself unattractive.

I told her how pleased I was to know that she blamed herself for trying to kill her brother out of sibling rivalry. Since every part of the trauma outline is irrational, this was proof that this wasn't actually true. This realization brought her great relief. After clearing the trauma, we muscle tested for the real reason she dropped her baby brother. It was an accident. Abigail left the session encouraged to start dating again.

HOW I TREAT PEOPLE FOR TRAUMA

There are many different methods that work to release trauma from the body. I'm trained in NLP, applied kinesiology, and energy psychology techniques, so I use approaches from this repertoire. For trauma, my clients principally use the NBD technique for all the associated negative emotions and limiting beliefs that compose a trauma outline.

NBD is similar to EFT. Techniques that use this approach are now generally known as meridian tapping techniques, or "tapping." I have included the protocol for combining knowledge of the trauma outline with the use of the NBD technique in Chapter 8. My procedures are merely suggestions, and I recommend that professionals assist in healing traumatized clients by using what works in their own repertoire.

If you understand the trauma outlines and learn how to do Natural Bio-Destressing, *can you treat trauma yourself?*

Yes, if it's a simple trauma. The Do-It-Yourself Protocol for Treating Trauma is in Chapter 8. As soon as you get bad news or have an injury, treat yourself right then. For more severe and layered trauma (described at the end of this chapter), I recommend you work with a trained professional.

The first step. I ask the client to recall the memory where they experienced the trauma, decide if it's a loss or violence trauma (or both), and read the trauma outline. I ask the client to notice what emotions or beliefs come up for them, where in their body they feel it, run the scene again in their minds, and treat with a round of NBD. Usually, clients choose to start with the initial shock and fear (I. A. Shock/Fear), but sometimes, anger, shame, or another emotion might be dominant. If the client bursts out in tears just thinking about it, it's probably sadness and grief. We start with whatever feeling or belief comes up first, or whatever is most intense.

Often, when we start by clearing the feeling of shock or fear, it unfreezes the memory so the client can then easily access the emotions in the rest of the pattern.

The emotions of anger/rage, sadness, and hurt (Category I. B-D) will often surface immediately after the initial shock/fear is cleared. While frozen, it's common for people to be unaware that they carry those emotions at all or feel them with such intensity. In a loss, the anger/rage, sadness, and hurt are often directed at the person who left. "I feel angry/sad/hurt that you left me/how could you leave me?" In a violence imprint the feelings are often about what happened.

For example, Lucy, age 44, came to see me because she was diagnosed with stage four liver cancer. Lucy seemed very upbeat and cheerful as she told me about her diagnosis, how the doctors told her there was no treatment, and her life expectancy was now three months. Then she told me, "I always wanted to have a baby. When I was 42, I had a baby girl."

Puzzled as to why she seemed so upbeat and cheerful, I asked, "Since things seem to be going so well for you, why have you come to see me?"

"My husband is having a really hard time dealing with this situation," she replied. She told me he was not all that capable of a man, and that she was afraid he wouldn't survive without her.

I gently explained to Lucy that she was in shock, and it was masking a deep grief. We went back to the scene where she received the diagnosis, concentrated on the shock, and started tapping. Halfway through the tapping process, she started crying and remarked with surprise, "You were right; there really is a lot of grief here."

Sometimes, a person is hesitant to enter a traumatic memory. I direct them to begin tapping while thinking about the event from a distance. When some of the charge has cleared from a distance, the client can then relate to emotions in the scene and finish clearing the whole trauma.

Sometimes, I feel hesitant to ask a person to recall a memory, particularly in cases of sexual violence. I worked by phone with a client three days after she experienced attempted rape at gunpoint. She was afraid to leave her apartment, was unable to sleep, and spent much of her time trembling and crying. I apologized for asking her to remember what happened.

"I've flashed back into the memory over the last several days, many times for no good reason," she said. "I don't mind recalling the memory once more for a good reason." Immediately after the intervention, she stopped shaking and crying, was able to sleep, and went to work the next day.

People who've experienced severe and/or repetitive violence (often starting in childhood) with or without a sexual component, or who have blocked memories, should ***only treat this with a professional*** (see description of levels of severity of trauma at the end of this chapter).

The intermediate steps. After the priority emotion is cleared, the remainder of the imprint may be cleared in any order except for the anticipatory phobia, which is cleared last (see below). The other pieces of the pattern come up in order of priority for that individual. When a client no longer feels any negativity associated with that memory, I muscle test each line of the trauma outline to confirm that everything is cleared. Muscle testing is a standard technique in applied kinesiology and energy psychology for speaking directly to the unconscious, body, and soul levels of a person. To practitioners trained in NLP or hypnosis, muscle testing looks like ideomotor signaling, i.e., consistent unconscious body movements (usually of the fingers) signifying yes or no answers. (See instructions for muscle testing in Chapter 8.)

In situations where there was violence in the home, clients often have difficulty accessing the anger/rage part of the imprint, even after the initial shock/fear is cleared. They're afraid to express anger toward the attacker for fear of attracting or provoking another attack. In reality, it's actually safer for children to hide, freeze, and become invisible, or run away from violence occurring between other members of the household than it is to remain. Unfortunately, the fear of expressing anger generalizes into beliefs such as, "It's not okay to feel angry," "I can't let people know when I feel angry," or "I can't express my anger safely and appropriately."

In addition, the children who run to a neighbor or relative often feel guilty of cowardice and for not protecting the recipient of violence. Clients need to be cleared of their fear of anger and their guilt over the natural instinct for self-preservation before they can clear the anger toward the perpetrator. I find that NBD works well here.

A client who was having marital problems reported that she was haunted by the memory of a violence incident in which she let a man posing as a customer into her store, whom she "shouldn't have let in" ("It's my fault because."). As soon as she spoke these words, she burst into tears and started shaking (she flashed back or associated into the memory). I directed her to start the NBD technique, to concentrate on the fear, and to "learn what she needed to learn in a way that served her highest good."

She stopped crying after one round and said, "I realize it's not my fault." After a second round of NBD, she reported, "I realize that I did have some control (she cleared "I'm powerless and have no control") over the situation because although he threatened me with a weapon, I convinced him not to rape me by telling him I was having my period." Instead, he forced her to perform oral sex.

At this point, she interrupted the session to go wash out her mouth (feeling of pollution). At the next session, she reported she repeated the NBD technique in the evening after our first session, cried all night, and no longer experienced sadness associated with the memory (cleared sadness). Furthermore, she decided it would be in her best interest to clear the rest of this imprint before she and her husband started couples counseling.

Feeling Vulnerable/Boundary Violation or Breach can be easily repaired with NBD.

The Feeling of Pollution can be easily repaired with NBD. It can also be cleared with smudging. This is a Native American ritual in which the practitioner lights a wand of sage and encircles the client with smoke from foot to head in order to "drive away the evil spirits" that have touched him. You can even buy smudge spray, which alleviates the need for the smoke. I have found this intervention to be successful in every case in which I used it, although I'm still mystified about how it works.

All other limiting beliefs in Category II, as well as additional limiting beliefs for that client and that specific trauma, are cleared well with NBD.

Dead Parts often must be found with muscle testing because they don't talk or feel like anything.

Even if you aren't using muscle testing, you can hear a person describe a dead part when they report, "When __________ happened (i.e., my wife died suddenly), I felt dead inside, I felt like a zombie, I feel like the best part of me died, I've never been the same since." For physical injury or illness traumas, a physical dead part is a part of the body that has lost function. For example, in diabetes, the pancreas that is no longer functioning registers as a dead part.

I worked with a client who muscle tested for a dead part, and when I asked her where she felt it, she said she didn't feel anything.

"Of course not," I said. "That's because it thinks it's dead. Where is the non-feeling feeling?"

"Oh," she said, "it's right here," and pointed to her stomach.

Anticipatory phobia, the last step. If there's no underlying root cause for a loss (e.g., death or loss by accident, parents got divorced), we clear the anticipatory phobia when the client decides that it has priority. However, losses in relationships or business and experiences of violence may stem from unresolved emotional issues from a person's past. In these cases, we clear the anticipatory phobia with the NBD technique *after* we have cleared the root cause and preferably all the other categories.

The reasoning behind this order is that after clearing the trauma imprint, the individual will have eliminated issues at the unconscious and body level that could have led to the regeneration of the pattern. It's then reasonable to expect that it will not happen again, and it's not necessary to carry persistent dread about the possibility that a similar event might happen at random. We then discuss 1) what it means to be "reasonably cautious," 2) that it's not necessary to feel fear in order to be cautious, and 3) rational solutions to potential problems.

Recent trauma imprints are often more severe if the person carries imprints from previous experiences (stacking or accumulation) of imprints. Of my five clients with cancer or precancerous cellular changes, all had a trauma imprint prior to, and similar to, a trauma imprint that preceded the onset of disease. Interestingly, if this isn't the first time the person has had this type of trauma, the imprint from all other examples of this pattern clears simultaneously forward and backward in time as we treat the trauma we have identified. As my clients clear trauma, I direct them to learn everything they need to learn to serve their highest good.

Since traumatic events are often unpredictable, I train clients to perform the NBD technique so they're empowered to protect themselves. They can actually prevent the onset of a trauma imprint while the event is in progress by using NBD (i.e., during a telephone call with bad news or during dental surgery). Alternatively, they can minimize any damage by clearing the pattern as soon as possible after it occurs.

Balanced Versus Unbalanced Emotions

An unbalanced emotion is an exaggerated and irrational emotion that comes from trauma (or other emotional damage patterns). A balanced emotion is an emotion that is reasonable and appropriate to feel under the circumstances. Sometimes after clearing a trauma, people still feel angry or sad, or some other negative emotion related to the event. The protocol for clearing trauma releases irrational and exaggerated emotions stuck in a person's nervous system, but it's not meant to turn people into unfeeling robots. Any emotion that remains after treating trauma is a balanced emotion appropriate to the situation and a sign that the individual needs to take some kind of action in reality to process the remaining emotion or deal with a real problem.

What kind of traumas can you treat yourself, and what kind of traumas require help from a professional?

In the decades since I published my first paper on trauma, I discovered that there are different levels of trauma severity, and several other types of trauma that contain the structure of loss and violence trauma within, but with a larger structure and specific variations. More severe degrees of trauma must be treated by a professional, preferably trained in HBLU™, NLP, EMDR, EFT, or other energy psychology-related healing methods that clear trauma from the body, and who understands that clearing severe trauma is a multi-step process.

I have included a discussion of more severe degrees of trauma so you can recognize these types of patterns and know when to seek appropriate professional help.

LEVELS OF SEVERITY OF TRAUMA

LEVEL 1: SIMPLE TRAUMA

In this book, I describe the structure of simple traumas common to everyday life that you can treat a lot of yourself. Common loss traumas include physical injury traumas, loss trauma from deaths, lost relationships, jobs, opportunities, illnesses and health challenges, rejection, betrayal, abandonment, life disappointments, and failures. Common violence traumas include initiating a relationship breakup, theft, getting yelled at or criticized, and verbal or physical assault.

LEVEL 2: FRAGMENTATIONS

If a trauma is more severe or intense than a simple trauma, it can cause individuals' personalities to fragment off or exile a part (a split) or parts (a multiple) of themselves. I rarely find fragmentations associated with loss, but I frequently find them associated with violence. Parts that split off are traumatized and can no longer perform their functions. One diagnostic indicator of fragmentation is a change in personality when someone drinks. The split-off part gets access to the person and takes over the behavior. This category of trauma includes ancestral trauma, including the ancestral death-wish pattern that causes depression and addictions (4, 5), and past life traumas that may require "soul retrieval," i.e., recovery of a split-off part of them.

LEVEL 3: BLOCKED MEMORIES

Sometimes a fragmentation is so severe that it triggers a protective mechanism in the unconscious mind, which I call the blocking mechanism. Like an electrical circuit, if there is a sufficiently intense surge of traumatic emotion, the blocking part flips a circuit breaker that blocks the conscious mind from accessing the traumatic memory or memories of that part of his/her life for fear that conscious awareness of the trauma would overwhelm and paralyze the conscious mind.

Although the intention of the blocking mechanism is to keep you sane and functioning, the client still experiences mental, emotional, and physical symptoms of trauma, but has no way to connect with and clear them. Some common traumas that people block include sexual violence and severe or chronic trauma. I developed a protocol for eliminating PTSD symptoms in 1- 6 sessions (published in two peer-reviewed case studies) (6,7).

LEVEL 4: AUTONOMOUS PARTS

The most severe form of trauma results in autonomous parts—parts that fragmented off, blocked, or walled off. Examples include neglect trauma (which causes attachment disorder) and attempted physical murder trauma.

Although these mechanisms protect the person as a whole, they prevent access to the full range of functions available when all the parts are healthy and working together.

HBLU™ methodology has effective protocols for healing all levels of trauma. I recommend anything above the level of a simple trauma be treated with an HBLU™ or equivalent trained professional.

CONCLUSION

In the years since I published this original study, I have found that the characteristics of loss and violence traumas have remained constant in all the clients I treated. During the process of clearing trauma imprints, many clients learned to recognize the patterns and respect the resulting degree of damage in themselves and others. When they learned the skills necessary to clear trauma, they developed a sense of confidence in their ability to transcend life's accidents and tragedies. The long-term reproducibility and success of this protocol allow me to conclude that trauma damage can be healed at the conscious, unconscious, body, and soul levels.

I also developed protocols for treating trauma of all levels of severity and trained many people in this method. The people I've trained get the same results I do. I have presented the protocol for treating simple trauma to many mental health and healing professionals at conferences and trainings (8). This method is being recognized as a standard protocol to understand and treat trauma and help people make progress in areas of their lives where previously they were unable to progress. My hope in publishing this book is to empower more people to prevent and/or release trauma as soon as possible so that we all can live our best lives possible.

CHAPTER 3

PHYSICAL EFFECTS OF EMOTIONAL TRAUMA

Many people are aware that, somehow, vaguely, stress can cause physical symptoms such as headaches, high blood pressure, and digestive issues. In this chapter, I give specific examples of the kinds of physical symptoms directly caused by trauma and how treating the trauma cleared these symptoms.

PART 1: I CAN'T BREATHE

CLIENT 1

After the first client of the day, I walked out of my treatment office to find the head of the company who cleans our offices sitting in my waiting room.

Confused, I asked, "What are you doing here?"

"I came to find out how satisfied you are with the cleaning services," she replied.

"We're very happy with the cleaning services," I said.

When she didn't move, I sat down across from her and figured I'd do a little visiting. Her business was fine. Her children were fine. Then (since I had been to her wedding three years prior), I asked about her handsome husband. She informed me that eight months prior, she returned from caring for her ailing mother to discover that he had sold her condo, cleaned out all their bank accounts, and fled the country. "His sister doesn't even know where he is," she told me.

Immediately afterward, she experienced difficulty breathing. She went to her internist and then saw a cardiologist because she was afraid something was wrong with her heart. No one could find anything physically wrong with her. Puzzled, she added, "And I feel angry with my kids and my employees all the time."

I immediately invited her into my treatment office, explained trauma to her, and began doing NBD. Three rounds later, she could breathe and no longer felt angry. When asked how she felt now, she said, "I'll be alright," and, "This is a really great technique." Her cleaning business is still flourishing.

CLIENT 2

The following is a letter a client sent to her doctor after I treated her.

Dear Doctor,

Yesterday I was treated by Judith Swack, who developed HBLU™ Healing from the Body Level Up™. I had emailed her my symptoms. She said that when a person can't breathe that usually indicates a loss trauma.

The weekend before the breathlessness started, I visited my 18-year-old daughter who is working as a camp counselor in the San Juan Islands. She will be going away to college in the fall. When I left her this time, I knew when I saw her in a few weeks she would no longer be a child but pretty much an adult. I would be losing my baby forever.

We cleared this with TAT, a holding method that releases emotions from your body, but it would not completely clear. This is because I had an earlier loss trauma. This occurred when Erin was six years old. One day when I looked at my six-year-old, I realized my baby was gone. That little person I was so in love with had disappeared.

The method of choice to clear this was psychic observation. This is where Judith just looks at you and sees what she sees. What she saw was a Valentine-type heart cracked in half and hanging on by a thread. She told me to pick it up and mold it back together, which I did—figuratively of course. She watched as it turned from a dark color to a bright red. She said it carried the love of God, which was mine to hold but not to keep.

The learning I took away from this is to love the whole person, not just the three-year-old or the 16-year-old. Although this may sound very strange, my breathing is completely back to normal. The amount of medication or lack of medication I have taken has no effect on my breathing. This is a BIG relief.

This loss trauma is very common in women with only one child. Occasionally, it happens when there are two or more children. If you don't mind, I will keep you posted when I run into something like this. The jury is still out on my new medication. I will let you know.

Thanks. L.C.

CLIENT 3

The following is a testimonial a client sent after I treated her.

In 2003, while traveling by car to visit my sister, who was very ill, we stopped for construction on the interstate highway and were hit from behind by a truck going full speed. The resulting impact caused the car to catch fire. We were both rescued before the fire got us, and we thought we were okay, other than a few cuts, bumps, and bruises.

The next night, my husband had a massive stroke from a torn and leaking artery, which was not found by the emergency room doctors, leaving him in bad shape. He had lost most of his left-brain function, including 80% or more of comprehension, plus all speaking, reading, writing, even gesturing, as well as almost all right-side function. As a result, as he improved to the point of understanding the condition he was in, he became suicidally depressed.

Over the past five years, he progressed well, despite dire predictions from physicians. We tried every option for improving his recovery chances, traditional and alternative. Due to those efforts, he went from being completely dependent to living a fairly normal life with some physical handicaps. At this point, we were referred to Judith Swack to deal with the remaining emotional and physical trauma.

As we treated my experience of the trauma, I realized in that moment, I felt I had lost everything, including my husband, our wonderful life together, and my joy in being alive. My husband and I have a very special relationship that few married people, I believe, are fortunate to have—we delight in each other, even after many years together. We are partners in everything. What this accident did was devastating to me… to us.

To clear the shock and fear, my deepest wisdom called for Judith to channel healing energy into my body. She said it looked like a cannonball had been shot through the center of my chest, leaving a gaping black hole. My lungs were squeezed against the sides of my chest and looked like rubber chickens. I told her I hadn't been able to breathe normally since the accident. My lungs felt so heavy. The sadness I felt was palpable. It seemed to block oxygen from getting to my lungs, to the point of being painful, when something triggered acute memories of our pre-accident life.

After a few minutes, she reported seeing the hole close up and the lungs drop down and inflate. I could actually breathe again! It's been three months, and I'm still breathing comfortably and can feel the difference in my level of inner peace. Thank you, Judith, for helping me be comfortable in my body again.

K.W., Retired Systems Engineer

People hold their breath when they're frightened. As I treat people for trauma, I know the emotion we're working on has cleared when they take a deep breath.

PART 2: HBLU™ CAN SUCCESSFULLY TREAT INFERTILITY

All living things want to reproduce, and most people expect that they will grow up and have a family and children of their own. When people have difficulty conceiving, it's very troubling. They start to doubt their masculinity or femininity. They start to worry that if they can't reproduce, their partner will leave them. They may even feel they have no value as a person if they don't have children. This is historically truer for women than for men.

Infertility is a very traumatic situation. People who want to have children and have trouble conceiving feel disappointed and traumatized by their perceived failure. In fact, I object to doctors calling themselves "infertility specialists." Who wants to see a doctor who can help them become infertile? I think they should call themselves "fertility specialists"! I've treated several women for infertility, and not surprisingly, emotional trauma can cause physical infertility.

Amy Goldblum was a nice, 23-year-old Jewish law student when she met George Yang, a nice, 32-year-old Chinese astronomy graduate student at an open house at the observatory. She asked him if he would show her galaxies through the telescope, but he said it takes 24 or more hours of filming to see them. Nonetheless, she thought he was cute and polite, so she invited him to a party at her house the following week. Not much of a drinker, Amy decided, since the party was at her house and she didn't have to drive home, she'd have a drink or three. George stayed until the end of the party and offered to help clean up. He ended up sleeping over.

Amy and George continued to date, and a couple of months later, Amy discovered she was pregnant. She felt she was too young and at too early a stage in her career to get married and have a baby. George said whatever she decided, he would support her. Amy had an abortion. Eventually, they broke up, and George married a nice Chinese art student. After that, Amy religiously practiced birth control.

After having established herself in a successful law practice, Amy, 36, met and married Irwin Schwartz, a nice, Jewish accountant. After buying their first home, they were ready to start a family. By then, Amy was 39 years old, but didn't think she'd have a problem getting pregnant. A year and a half later, Amy was still not pregnant, so they went for fertility testing. Irwin tested fertile.

For Amy's first test, a hysterosalpingogram, her obstetrician injected a dye through the cervix, which would normally move up the fallopian tubes (the tubes the sperm travel through to get to the egg) to the ovaries. The pathway could be seen on an X-ray. In Amy's case, the dye did not travel up, indicating the fallopian tubes were blocked.

Her obstetrician recommended a second test: a laparoscopy, a surgical procedure where she could examine the fallopian tubes from inside the body. Again, the obstetrician found the fallopian tubes were blocked.

"Why did I need a second test when the first showed a blockage?" Amy asked. "The fallopian tubes are lined with smooth muscle," her doctor replied. "Sometimes, when you inject dye, the tubes react by spasming shut. I needed to follow up with a visual check." Amy's doctor continued, "It will be impossible to get pregnant the normal way. You'll have to do *in vitro* fertilization."

On the doctor's advice, Amy and Irwin consulted a fertility specialist and left the fertility clinic feeling disgusted and discouraged.

Amy knew arteries were lined with smooth muscle and had read that mind-body techniques, such as meditation, could lower blood pressure. She reasoned that if mind-body techniques could relax smooth muscle in the arteries, they could relax smooth muscle in the fallopian tubes. So, Amy came for HBLU™ therapy with the goal of getting pregnant "the normal way."

We discovered that the abortion trauma was the highest priority interference to Amy getting pregnant, and we cleared it in one session. We discovered that Amy was so angry with herself for "accidentally" getting pregnant that she made a limiting decision to punish herself if she ever got pregnant again, and her body shut down her fallopian tubes.

Amy got pregnant the normal way two weeks later.

Amy took a drugstore pregnancy test and happily called her doctor's office with the news. The receptionist told her to come in and have a regular blood test. That was also positive.

Amy heard nothing from the doctor's office, so she called again and asked, "Am I supposed to make an appointment for some kind of prenatal care?" The receptionist said, "The doctor doesn't believe the blood test results and wants you to return for a second test."

The second test was positive.

Again, there was no call from the doctor's office. Amy called again and asked, "Should I make an appointment for prenatal care?" The receptionist repeated that the doctor didn't believe the blood test results and was certain, *because she had seen it with her own eyes*, that it was impossible for Amy to be pregnant. And if she were pregnant, then it must be an ectopic pregnancy, so Amy should get an immediate ultrasound.

Amy went for an ultrasound. When the ultrasound technician asked if Amy was having any bleeding, cramping, or other unusual symptoms, Amy replied, "No, I'm here because my doctor doesn't believe I'm really pregnant." The ultrasound showed a normal embryo growing in the uterus, right where it should be. The technician said she'd send the results to the doctor's office and gave Amy a picture.

After a week with no call from the doctor's office, Amy called again and asked, "Should I make an appointment for prenatal care?" When the receptionist wasn't sure what to do, Amy said, "Are you telling me to find another obstetrician?" The receptionist hastily checked with the doctor and made an appointment for Amy.

A week later, Amy went for her first prenatal checkup. The doctor entered the room, her face expressionless and white as a sheet. Her first words were, "What did you do?"

Amy, realizing the doctor was in shock, thought quickly and said, "I got pregnant the normal way, and I have you to thank for that."

"What do you mean?" the doctor asked, rousing herself.

Amy explained, "Well, you told me that the fallopian tubes are coated with smooth muscle and could spasm shut. There's research that shows mind-body techniques, such as meditation, have been shown to lower blood pressure by relaxing vascular smooth muscle. I figured smooth muscle, schmooze muscle, it's all the same, and I should be able to open the tubes with mind-body techniques. So, I went to an HBLU™ practitioner, had one session, and conceived naturally two weeks later." The doctor visibly shook herself, the color returning to her face, and said, "Well, whatever the case, you're pregnant now, so let's get on with it."

Amy had an uneventful pregnancy. She met all five obstetricians in her doctor's practice because they rotated delivering the babies of all patients in the practice. Amy still preferred that her baby be delivered by her own obstetrician, so a week before she was due, she asked her doctor what day she was scheduled to do deliveries. Her baby was due on April 27, and her doctor was on call for April 28. So, Amy informed her doctor that she would arrange with her baby to be delivered on the 28th.

Amy asked her doctor what time of day would be most convenient for her to do the delivery, and her doctor suggested between 3:00 and 4:00 p.m. Amy replied that she'd arrange things with her baby. She used an HBLU™ technique to communicate with her baby, and sure enough, Barbara was born healthy, happy, and alert at 3:30 p.m. on April 28.

Remember, your body is *your* body. You are the customer paying doctors for their services. If you don't understand what they're talking about or why they're making certain suggestions, ask more questions. If you're not comfortable with that provider, find another one. Taking care of your body is a team effort with you as the team leader.

PART 3: ALLERGIES

I never thought my mother, a big fan of Western medicine, was particularly interested in or supportive of my mind-body healing method. After she died, my father surprised me by telling me that she always believed in my work. "What makes you think so, Dad, since she was never willing to work with me?"

"It's because you cured your allergies," he replied. "She used to hear you wheezing every night (through two closed bedroom doors and a hallway in between), and suddenly it stopped." Although she took me to many doctors, arranged for weekly allergy shots, and gave me all the prescription medication available at that time, my mother felt bad that it wasn't really helping. She was really impressed that all my symptoms cleared in one session.

Here is my story.

My earliest memories are from age three, lying in bed in the summertime, wheezing and sweating. I had severe hay fever and asthma starting at the beginning of July through the first frost in autumn. I tested positive for allergies to summer grasses, Alternaria (a kind of mold), and ragweed. I had weekly allergy shots, took antihistamines and stimulants, and slept on an elevated pillow to no avail. I could not go to overnight camp because I couldn't breathe at night. These were the days before air conditioning and air purifiers, so I just suffered every summer.

When I was 21 years old, medical science finally developed an inhaler of a powder that prevented allergic asthma reactions and actually worked. I felt saved. I still needed shots and medication for the rest of my symptoms.

At age 30, I saw an NLP therapist for help with relationships. She happened to be a nurse who specialized in rebirthing. One day, she remarked that I was "hard to reach" emotionally, so I suggested we work on that. She asked me, "What comes to mind when you think about that subject?" I immediately thought of my birth.

My mother frequently regaled me with the fact that she had had a beautiful fantasy about bringing me (her first child) into the world through natural childbirth. She refused medication and was determined to have the full experience. Unfortunately, she couldn't push me out. She was in labor for 24 hours, and I was stuck inside. Finally, the doctor, noticing that she was weakening, decided to put her to sleep and just get me out. Since my father wasn't allowed in the delivery room, and my mother was asleep, we actually don't know what time I was born.

My therapist led me in a guided meditation where I imagined being stuck in the womb and suffocating. No one could reach me, and I was going to die. Then she told me to notice that there were two angels keeping me company, and they would make sure I got out safely. I felt instant relief and visualized being born easily.

That afternoon, I returned to work and noticed that my claustrophobia in elevators was completely gone! For some reason, I also stopped arguing with my boss. Even more astonishing, all my allergy symptoms disappeared! That year, on our regular family summer vacation to a cabin in Maine, I was able to sleep and be out in nature with no symptoms. I got through ragweed season without a sneeze. I haven't had an allergic reaction for decades.

I never could understand why clearing birth trauma cleared my allergies until my friend, the famous Norma Feldman, said, "Judith, it's obvious." When is your birthday? I was born on June 30th, and because of birth trauma, I reacted to any pollen that was in the air at that time. It's true that I never reacted to spring tree or grass pollen, only to summer pollens. The allergies were that specific.

Although I unintentionally cleared my allergy symptoms as a positive side effect of clearing trauma, I have since helped people clear their allergic symptoms by clearing the trauma that started them. I discuss the neurobiological mechanisms of treating allergies in Chapter 6.

As you can see from these examples, emotional trauma can cause physical symptoms in the body. Attempts to treat these kinds of symptoms with physical interventions are often not very effective because the *cause of the symptoms is not physical.* Muscle testing allows you to distinguish physical from emotional causes so you can treat the symptoms appropriately and effectively.

CHAPTER 4

SPECIFIC TYPES OF LOSS

Most people recognize death or a romantic relationship breakup as a loss trauma. There are many other, more subtle, but just as powerful, experiences of loss, and it's important to recognize these traumas and treat them. In this chapter I describe the loss traumas that occur when a person gets a diagnosis of a serious illness (diagnosis shock), loses a job (job loss trauma), has teenagers leave for college (empty nest transition trauma), has a near death experience, leaves young children for too long a period of time causing separation anxiety, and of course, birth trauma.

PART 1: DIAGNOSIS SHOCK: THE UNRECOGNIZED BURDEN OF ILLNESS

I first published this paper in 2008 with the intention of helping patients, families of patients, and healthcare professionals prevent or minimize the trauma of discovering there is a possibility that someone has a serious illness, or actually has a serious illness. I named this type of trauma "diagnosis shock." On my website, I state, **"Please give copies of this paper to all your friends and healthcare providers!"** You can find the reference with the link as the last note (33) for this chapter. In this book, I added more recent additional research at the end of this chapter.

WHAT IS DIAGNOSIS SHOCK?

Diagnosis shock is the phobic reaction people experience the moment they first suspect or are told that they have a serious physical or emotional illness. Many researchers have found that people who are diagnosed with a serious illness experience shock and trauma, which in some cases can even lead to mental illness such as depression and anxiety (1-20). Many researchers have made excellent suggestions for minimizing the severity of diagnosis shock and for psychologically supporting people and their families who have been diagnosed with a severe illness (1, 2, 4, 11, 12, 13, 15, 17, 19, 20).

The purpose of the 2008 paper was to help patients and healthcare professionals recognize, prevent, and treat diagnosis shock. It contains the results of over 12 years of experience in treating people for diagnosis shock. This paper is the first report of the use of energy psychology techniques to successfully prevent and (if necessary) clear diagnosis shock from the *unconscious mind* and *body.*

This study involved over 100 people with a variety of health-related problems who came for treatment with Healing from the Body Level Up™ (HBLU™) methodology (21). Each client was taught to access information from the unconscious mind using the NLP technique of going inside and talking to the part that needs healing. Clients were taught to recognize unconscious communication as visual, auditory, or kinesthetic signals. Each client was also taught to access information from the body level using the applied kinesiology technique of muscle testing, in which the body registers true or false answers to questions through differences in muscle strength.

Clients with diagnosis shock described their conscious reactions and then were questioned using muscle testing to determine their reactions at the unconscious and body levels. Treatment for the negative emotions and limiting beliefs found in diagnosis shock-associated traumatic reactions was done using energy psychology techniques. Each client was followed for one to six months after treatment.

EXAMPLES OF DIAGNOSIS SHOCK

Mary

After a routine mammogram, Mary received a postcard requesting that she return for another mammogram. Hysterical, she cancelled all social engagements for the next month (including a visit to her son and his family for Christmas) and refused to even leave her house. One month later, she repeated her mammogram. It was normal.

Joe

Blood tests taken at his yearly physical exam revealed that Joe had very high PSA levels, a diagnostic test used to detect prostate cancer. After a biopsy confirmed the diagnosis, Joe insisted he had no anxiety and that he didn't need to research treatment options because he believed his spirituality would cure him. Instead, he wanted to focus on making more money. His denial that he was upset and his magical thinking indicated he was in shock.

Frank

Frank had bladder cancer. He met a woman who claimed she'd cured herself of cancer simply by eating a raw food diet. Frank decided that if this regimen worked for her, it would work for him. He began the diet and stopped all further treatment. One day, he ate a cookie. The next day, he was overcome with terror that his cancer would return, and he would now die because he violated his diet.

Samantha

Samantha was diagnosed with (and hospitalized several times for) bipolar disorder in her 30s. Now over 50, she had never been married, lived in a condo she disliked, and dreamed of retiring from teaching to start her own business. Yet Samantha refused to take any medication for her problem.

Angela

Angela's gynecologist discovered a breast lump during an annual exam and recommended that she make an appointment with the receptionist for a mammogram. As she left the examining room, she began to feel faint. She collapsed in the waiting room and hit her head on a table. Angela spent the rest of the day in the emergency room under observation for a head injury. Her mammogram was normal.

The irrational reactions of these people were caused by ***diagnosis shock***.

HOW DO PEOPLE GET DIAGNOSIS SHOCK?

Diagnosis shock *always* occurs when a medical professional diagnoses someone as having a serious illness, whether physical or psychological in nature. I've even found diagnosis shock may occur when a medical professional suggests a diagnostic test for a serious condition or asks for more testing because of unclear results. Surprisingly, in some people, diagnosis shock occurs through a process of self-diagnosis, i.e., a person notices unexplained symptoms and self-diagnoses the possibility of something terribly wrong. Note that even clients who have no physical ailments or symptoms can have diagnosis shock.

WHAT HAPPENS IN THE MOMENT OF INITIAL SHOCK?

What my clients and I found when we explored the reaction at the moment of initial shock was that they ask themselves consciously or unconsciously, "What could this ___ (news or symptom) possibly mean?" The unconscious mind instantly generates a worst-case scenario of loss and death so vivid, extreme, and frightening that it triggers a fight-or-flight reaction. People usually experience this reaction as an intense adrenaline rush of fear, a feeling of frozenness or numbness, and/or a sharp indrawn breath followed by an inability to breathe normally, think clearly, or hear anything that's said afterwards. Exclamations like "I don't believe it," or "It can't be true," are common. Anything that was in the environment at the time can become associated with that memory and later trigger flashbacks to the original event. These exaggerated, irrational, emotional, and physical responses occur so rapidly that *some people are not even consciously aware they're in shock.*

In the case of cancer, the unconscious mind runs through scenarios of painful and ultimately ineffective treatment leading to death. In the case of heart disease-related symptoms, the unconscious mind goes right to scenarios of unpredictable and sudden death. Suspicion of autoimmune diseases, such as multiple sclerosis, leads the unconscious mind to an inevitable outcome of physical helplessness and being trapped in a paralyzed body. Any serious illness of the eyes leads to the unconscious conclusion of blindness. Strong emotional or mental reactions that seem different from others may lead a person's unconscious mind to conclude he is crazy.

Even if these suspicions turn out to be groundless, which they often do, diagnosis shock remains imprinted in the unconscious mind and body. Because it *feels* real, people react as if it *is* real! That's why the outward degree to which each person reacts does not correlate with whether or not they actually have an illness.

There are many different ways people attempt to cope with diagnosis shock, including:

- Panicking.
- Repressing or denying the fear.
- Attempting to talk oneself out of it: "I don't believe it," "That's ridiculous," "It's probably nothing," "That can't be real," "I'm not really worried," "I'll be all right," "That's just my imagination."
- Attempting to dissipate the fear with magical thinking: "Someone or something will magically save me," "I believe in miracles," "A positive attitude will cure me."
- Distracting oneself by keeping busy or worrying about another person or topic.
- Avoiding dealing with the issue.
- Pretending the disease doesn't exist.
- Looking for constant reassurance from others.

These coping strategies do not get rid of the fear and, in fact, can cause added stress.

Casey

Casey was undergoing treatment for breast cancer. She believed that to survive cancer, she needed to have a positive attitude. Although she always appeared to be cheerful and optimistic, she couldn't sleep. She was afraid to feel or express negative emotions because she believed that:

- "If I admit I'm upset, my doctors and all medical personnel will dislike me, refuse to treat me, and I'll die."
- "If I admit I'm upset, my friends will reject me, and I'll die alone."
- "If I feel any upset, the negativity will kill me." Patients with this belief may withdraw, isolate themselves, and avoid support groups for fear that other people in the group may die and depress or frighten them out of their optimistic healing attitude.

Reactions to diagnosis shock can cause compliance problems, including failure to follow through on instructions or participate in prescribed treatment plans (3, 20). Avoidance, distraction, and magical thinking are more likely to kill a person than dealing rationally with what's going on. Furthermore, the continuous triggering of the body's fight-or-flight reaction suppresses the immune system (22) just at the time it needs to be strongest.

THE STRUCTURE OF DIAGNOSIS SHOCK IS A LOSS TRAUMA

My clients and I explore and treat different facets of diagnosis shock. In agreement with others (13, 20), we discovered that diagnosis shock is perceived as a loss trauma, the structure of which is summarized in Chapter 2. I begin treatment by asking people to remember the moment when they first suspected or discovered they might have a health problem. Because the reaction is phobic in nature, people easily (and vividly) recall the scene. I then ask people what they imagined they lost in that moment. They typically feel that in addition to their life, they lost other things, including their health, independence, livelihood/career, future, family, and the opportunity to share significant life events of loved ones. The emotional reactions to loss trauma include feelings of **shock, fear, anger, sadness**, and **hurt**.

There is **shame** about:

- Being sick (it wasn't too long ago that cancer was a secret, and mental illness was considered a sin)
- Feeling afraid (meaning weak or cowardly)
- Needing to depend on others for physical/emotional support and care during and after treatment

There is an incredible amount of **guilt** associated with diagnosis shock. Patients experience guilt for the trauma they feel they have caused their loved ones by having a bad diagnosis. For example, Mary, the woman who wouldn't leave the house after her questionable mammogram, felt terrible guilt about traumatizing her husband, whose previous wife had died of breast cancer. In addition, she was ashamed that anyone would find out she might have cancer and pity her.

Patients diagnosed with a terminal illness feel guilty that their loved ones will feel abandoned by their death. Patients with debilitating illnesses feel guilty for being a "burden" if they need outside help, support, and care. To compensate, they may continue taking care of others and carry on with business as usual when they really need to attend to themselves, and allow others to care for them so they can heal.

Along with the major negative emotions, people imprint a series of limiting beliefs, i.e., irrational beliefs, that they feel are true even though they're not. When individuals suffer a loss, they try to make sense of it, rationalize it, and understand why it happened. They try to figure out who or what is **responsible** for this tragedy. Who or what can they **blame**?

- **It's my fault because _________.** Some people blame their illness on risky behavior such as smoking. Others may believe they're being punished for past failures or mistakes.
- **It's other people's fault because _________.** People blame medical personnel and facilities, or other family members, for the problem. One woman who actually did have lung cancer

blamed her husband for causing her to smoke by telling her not to do it.

- **It's God's fault because _________.** People feel somehow punished, cheated, or betrayed by God, fate, or luck. They ask, "Why me?" There's an underlying expectation that some cosmic, all-powerful force should have been looking after them, but slipped up. People feel bitter, disappointed, and disconnected from God because of this. Some even report that they've stopped praying.

People who experience loss trauma worry about who will be there to meet their financial, emotional, physical, and social needs. They wonder: ***Who will take care of me?*** This question is especially charged for people with elderly spouses who may not be physically capable of doing the caretaking. There is also a feeling that "**People will leave me; I can't trust them,**" because others will be afraid of or repelled by their sickness. Individuals with this belief are unable to share their feelings or show their real selves to anyone for fear of alienating them. A variation of this is, "**My body has betrayed me; I can't trust it**."

During a traumatic loss, people feel, "**I am powerless or helpless/I have no control**" over the disease, the treatment program, or their lives. They may be unable to take charge of the situation. As one woman put it, "I don't know what chemotherapy the doctor is using. My husband keeps track of all that."

People may also feel, "**I am bad/unlovable/unwanted/undeserving/unworthy.**" This belief also comes in the form of, "I have no value." They believe the attention they're getting is, at some level, undeserved and unwarranted. They turn down offers of assistance or feel they must over-reciprocate for the love, friendship, and care they receive.

One of the distinguishing characteristics of a loss trauma is a **feeling of emptiness** or a sense of loss, that *something is missing*. It feels like an empty or hollow sensation in the heart or stomach. This sensation can trigger addictive behavior in which people try to fill the empty space with food or alcohol. One client said, "Since I'm going to die anyway, I may as well enjoy myself now," and subsequently developed a weight problem. The feeling of emptiness may also lead to depression. As another client put it, "I'd rather die than live like this."

Every trauma imprint comes with **anticipatory phobias**—fears that the traumatic event will happen again. The anticipatory phobia is characterized by a pervasive underlying feeling of dread. People with diagnosis shock often feel anxious about going to the doctor for fear of bad news. Even little symptoms or seemingly abnormal reactions trigger the fear that the illness has recurred. I call this the "Every little thing is cancer (or other illness)" pattern. One of my clients, who had a heart attack several years ago, panicked every time he experienced shortness of breath. After repeated testing showed his heart to be normal, his cardiologist prescribed a tranquilizer that not only calmed him down but also cleared his shortness of breath.

People may also experience other negative emotions, including bitterness, hate, and disgust. They may imprint additional limiting beliefs and irrational thoughts. They may develop limiting identities such as, "I'm a victim of this illness." They may make limiting decisions such as, "I have to stay away from doctors." They may feel that some part of them has died inside. If there's guilt, shame, or blame, they may need to forgive or make amends to themselves, God, and others. Sometimes a root cause needs to be treated, such as an earlier trauma, underlying belief, or self-destructive behavior that led to this problem.

DIAGNOSIS SHOCK MAKES IT HARD TO CHOOSE TREATMENT OPTIONS

Diagnosis shock is always worse for people whose illness diagnosis is confirmed. Although I use cancer as a common example, the pattern applies to people with other physical or psychological illnesses. When people get a diagnosis of cancer, they're usually traumatized so badly that they can't hear what the doctor has to say. Many doctors are aware of this, so they ask patients to bring a support person with them to the appointment. What they don't realize is that most people close enough to the patient to be a support person also go into shock (5, 6, 14, 17). Now, traumatized patients must make life-and-death treatment decisions while getting help from their traumatized support systems.

Very few people who receive a cancer diagnosis are trained as oncologists. Experts give patients many treatment options and opinions, then ask them to choose their own treatment. No matter what they decide, neither patients nor experts can guarantee a cure; doctors speak of five-year survival rates instead. Patients may experience such intense feelings of doubt, confusion, and overwhelm that they develop phobias about having these feelings. An example is, "I'm afraid to feel doubt or confusion because it means I made the wrong decision, and it will kill me." This phobic reaction may stimulate people to balk at any treatment whatsoever for fear of making a mistake. They may second-guess, obsess, or over-treat themselves in an attempt to cover all the bases. If the treatment is unsuccessful, the fact that the patient made the choice leads to more self-blame. This puts even more strain on their minds and bodies.

People who can tolerate doubt have a better quality of life. When I told my lively, determined 90-year-old aunt that I'd be at her 100th birthday party, she replied that she didn't know if she'd live to be 100 because, after all, she'd had breast cancer four times. This statement just strengthened my belief that it wouldn't be cancer that killed her.

Roberta

Roberta had a very aggressive form of breast cancer. She underwent surgery and one round of chemotherapy. Her doctor recommended another round of chemotherapy, but Roberta was too sick to do another round at the time. About a year later, the cancer returned. She began researching alternative treatments but couldn't decide what to do. I asked Roberta, "What does your oncologist have to offer?"

She told me, "I don't have an oncologist," and furthermore was unwilling to even visit the hospital oncology department. "It would depress me too much to even enter the building because after treatment, my doctor told me that if the cancer does come back, it will kill me."

I asked Roberta how her husband was responding to the situation. She said he wasn't doing very well, but his way of helping was to feed her a raw food diet and prepare all the meals. After clearing diagnosis shock, Roberta chose a clinic and went for treatment.

Sam

Sam got a diagnosis of leukemia. He didn't feel sick at all. He got several opinions about different types of chemotherapy, all of which would make him feel sick. Sam decided not to get treated for fear that the doctors were "being too aggressive" and trying to make him sick. He avoided treatment altogether for a year, during which time his blood count rose, and the leukemia invaded his bone marrow. After clearing diagnosis shock, he started treatment the following week.

Although **both Roberta and Sam are M.D.s**, their broad knowledge of medicine didn't prevent or help them cope with diagnosis shock.

Diagnosis shock interferes with doctor/patient cooperation.

Many people work well and respectfully with their doctors and healthcare providers. It's not uncommon, however, for shocked patients to blame their doctors for upsetting them (another form of "shoot the messenger" or the typical trauma response, "It's other people's fault because _________."). They think: *If only the doctor had told me my test results in person rather than over the telephone, or if only the doctor hadn't been so cold, used a nicer tone of voice, or been more sensitive, I wouldn't be so upset.*

In addition, some of the recommended treatment options, such as surgical removal, chemotherapy, and radiation, are extreme and shocking. Sometimes doctors aren't certain of the treatment plan, or inform patients that there's nothing they can do. Suddenly, patients don't trust the doctors they're depending on to save their lives. Sometimes doctors even become the enemy.

The fact is, ***there's no way to deliver this kind of bad news without shocking the patient.*** Unfortunately, most doctors don't know how to prevent or clear trauma from their patients when they deliver bad news. They're trained to treat physical, not psychological issues. Diagnosis shock causes a drain on medical personnel when anxious patients require constant reassurance that doesn't alleviate their fears.

Once, I even treated a doctor for patient shock. His patient had just recovered from a life-threatening crisis caused by an autoimmune disease. The caring doctor found a new medication that could reduce the severity of this kind of episode. He shared the good news by telling the patient that when she had a recurrence, she could use this new medication to minimize the effects. He went into shock when she became hysterical, screamed at him, called her husband into the office, and threatened to sue him. This doctor didn't understand that he had, in fact, suggested she'd have another episode of the illness, thus triggering the patient's anticipatory phobic reaction.

DIAGNOSIS SHOCK HURTS RELATIONSHIPS

Sonia and Frank

Sonia's husband, Frank, developed brain cancer and could no longer work. She got a job with enough flexibility to support the family and accompany her husband to his various treatments. Her husband's reaction to diagnosis shock was to withdraw emotionally and mentally. Sonia's reaction to diagnosis shock was to get so angry with Frank for abandoning her that she fought with him almost daily. Although she knew this was wrong, she couldn't control herself. Once we cleared her diagnosis shock, the fighting stopped.

John

John had a mild heart attack. After treatment, his doctor pronounced him fit enough to play baseball. His wife, however, stopped having sex with him for fear that any excitement or exertion might trigger another heart attack and kill him. We cleared John's diagnosis shock. He then explained to his wife that after two years without sex, he felt like he *wanted* to die. That week, they started having regular sex.

Gene

Gene's wife had breast cancer. He worried so much about losing her that he became distracted at work and imprinted *a second* loss trauma that his work performance would slip to the point that he'd be fired. He angrily blamed his wife for both his emotional discomfort and his imaginary job loss. After treating Gene for both loss traumas, the blaming stopped.

WHAT CAN HELP CLEAR DIAGNOSIS SHOCK?

After a phobic reaction like diagnosis shock has imprinted, no amount of facts or real information to the contrary can erase it. *Reality doesn't change a phobic reaction.* One study elegantly demonstrated this point when it compared the psychological symptoms of women with ductal carcinoma in situ (an easily treatable pre-cancerous condition) to the psychological symptoms of women with invasive cancer and found them to be identical (16)!

Thus, diagnosis shock must be cleared from the unconscious mind and body using a suitable technique. I found both Neuro-Linguistic Programming (NLP) and energy psychology techniques to be highly effective (24-31). I recommend using Natural Bio-Destressing (NBD), described in Chapter 8. NBD works by activating the nervous system's calming reflex to neutralize the fight-or-flight reflex, thus curing the phobic reaction (22, 33). NBD involves using the fingertips to tap on selected areas of the face, torso, and hands, and using eye movements and left-brain/right-brain integration techniques to resolve unpleasant memories.

You can treat yourself for Diagnosis Shock using the Do-It-Yourself Protocol for Treating Trauma in Chapter 8.

WHAT DO I RECOMMEND TO HEALTHCARE PROVIDERS?

One of the best things healthcare providers can do to minimize diagnosis shock is to use language carefully. This approach is supported by an article in *The New York Times*, "Doctors Learn How to Say What No One Wants to Hear" (1/10/06), which describes a $1.4 million program funded by the National Cancer Institute to train oncologists in how to communicate bad news to patients (35).

I developed the following communication guidelines for healthcare providers as a result of my 12-year study.

If a patient doesn't have any symptoms, the best way to suggest a test is:

- "Ms. Smith, I'd like you to get a blood test for _________ to make sure your _________ *is functioning normally*."
- "Ms. Smith, I'd like you to get a scan to confirm that the *therapy/treatment is working*."
- "Ms. Smith, you're due for your *routine test* (mammogram, EKG, cholesterol, etc.)."

If a patient has symptoms, the best way to suggest a test is:

- "Ms. Smith, I'd like you to do this test to rule out the possibility of anything serious."

When explaining the risks of a particular treatment, the best way to explain is:

- "In the past, a small percentage of people have experienced side effects like _________."
- If appropriate, add, "So we take the following measures _________ to minimize that possibility."

Refrain from giving the patient a definitive diagnosis until test results are back. Instead, say: "Let's find out what this is and then we'll come up with a treatment plan."

If after testing, a patient actually has a serious condition, I recommend the provider give the news in person and be sensitive about the use of language (see references 1 and 20 for excellent suggestions). Research by others (20) and myself has found that the proper environment and verbal technique alone can *minimize but not prevent* diagnosis shock. However, my clients, colleagues, and I have been able to *prevent diagnosis shock* by having the patient use one of the following techniques while listening to the news.

Healthcare providers can experience psychological distress when working with patients and their families. Now that you understand what both doctors and patients can experience during a traumatic diagnostic process, here are some simple techniques that can help you prevent diagnosis shock.

SIMPLE DIAGNOSIS SHOCK PREVENTION TECHNIQUES

1. Transformative Wholistic Reintegration (TWR): This technique was developed by Daniel Benor (34). I call it Hugging and Tapping. Do TWR by crossing your arms so that your hands rest on your biceps and tap alternately on each arm. The patient should do this technique for the first few minutes of the discussion, and better yet, for the entire medical appointment.
2. Natural Bio-Destressing (NBD): In the best of all possible worlds, I'd train every healthcare provider to help patients do NBD (see Figure 1) to clear any diagnosis shock before the patient leaves the office. I also recommend that healthcare providers (particularly nurses and medical social workers) do a round of NBD immediately after working with a difficult case and before leaving work for the day to prevent burnout.

WHAT DO I RECOMMEND TO MY CLIENTS?

Since I know any allusion to the topic of illness will trigger a phobic reaction and make it difficult to have a rational discussion, I start work with clients *by clearing diagnosis shock*. I teach clients and their families to do NBD. I recommend they treat themselves with NBD every morning for what they dread will happen that day, and every evening for anything that might have upset them during the day. I recommend using NBD before doctor's appointments on the anticipatory fear of bad news, using TWR (hugging and tapping) while talking with the doctor, and using NBD after each doctor's appointment to clear anything upsetting the doctor said.

I also recommend using NBD before any kind of treatment to clear the body's fear of invasion and harm. While performing the technique, I ask clients to convey the message to their bodies that this treatment is a healing intervention meant to make them well and to ask the body to fully receive the benefits of the treatment. This includes asking the body to send the treatment to where it's needed and to protect other parts of the body where the treatment is not needed.

Finally, I use NBD to clear feelings of doubt, uncertainty, and overwhelm.

FOLLOW-UP

After clearing diagnosis shock, I use the full range of techniques and protocols from the HBLU™ methodology to help people manage fear and diminish side effects during Western medical treatment, thus speeding healing. We clear any self-neglect, depression, and other self-destructive patterns that can interfere with proper self-care. In this way, HBLU™ treatment can even help extend life expectancy.

The end result of learning to manage your emotional and physical reactions with HBLU™ techniques includes:

- Reduced fear
- Feelings of empowerment
- Smoother doctor/patient relationships
- Fewer side effects
- Quicker recovery times
- More peace of mind
- Better quality of life

CAN WE PREVENT TRAUMA IN CASES WITH PREDICTABLE NEGATIVE OUTCOMES?

I did an experiment to answer that question. The answer is no and yes. Several of my clients' loved ones were diagnosed with terminal diseases such as cancer and Alzheimer's disease. We knew for certain these people would die within a predictable time frame. The question I wanted to answer was, if we treated my clients for diagnosis shock upon hearing about their loved one's condition, and treated them for what they imagined was going to happen, would that protect them from being traumatized at the actual event of their loved one's death?

The answer was that each client did imprint a loss trauma at the time of their loved one's death, but ***the degree to which they were traumatized was half as intense*** as it would have been, had we not treated them for diagnosis shock ahead of time.

Thus, I recommend everyone get treated for diagnosis shock.

PART 2: JOB LOSS TRAUMA

Job loss trauma can cause a tremendous amount of anxiety and physical and emotional symptoms of stress. It's important to recognize and treat job loss trauma to promote resilience, improve your chances of finding another job you actually want, and help you stay strong even in a traumatized economy.

TRAUMA CAN CAUSE IRRITABILITY

Janice and Frank

This scene really happened:

Janice (to husband Frank, the person in charge of carpooling): "Does Cathy (their daughter) have a debate tournament scheduled for this weekend?"

Frank: "No."

Janice: "Is Cathy scheduled for any activities this weekend?"

Frank: "Yes."

Janice (puzzled because swim season was over, and the only other activity that Cathy was involved in was debate): "So what is Cathy doing this weekend?"

Frank: "Debate."

Janice (surprised): "You just said she wasn't doing debate."

Frank: "Well, I thought you were talking about whether she had a home meet or an away meet."

Janice (certain there's something wrong with Frank): "You're being argumentative."

Frank: "No, I'm not."

Janice's first reaction was to get into a huge fight with Frank for being so difficult. But she realized this behavior was uncharacteristic of Frank, who's normally laid back and easy to get along with. Janice then realized he'd been argumentative, edgy, irritable, and at times almost hostile for the last three months. The timing of this behavior coincided with the start of layoffs at his company.

Naturally, Frank's manager assured everyone that there would be no layoffs in their department. And naturally, the company laid off people in Frank's department in the *first round* of layoffs, including the only person in the company who knew how to perform a vital product test. Each month thereafter, the company continued to lay off more people.

Exploring the reasons for Frank's uncharacteristic behavior, they realized (obviously in retrospect) that everybody in the company was anxious about losing their job and afraid the company was falling apart. Even if Frank himself wasn't laid off, it's still traumatic to lose friends and coworkers during layoffs, and Frank felt his own and everybody else's anxiety.

Both Janice and Frank knew the NBD technique for clearing traumatic shock, but *they hadn't thought to use it* because the shock he experienced was too subtle to recognize consciously! Now that they realized what was happening, Janice suggested Frank do NBD *every time he heard the word layoff.* Frank agreed and returned to being his good-natured self.

TRAUMA CAN CAUSE FEELINGS OF SHAKINESS AND TEARFULNESS

Simone and Roberta

During an HBLU™ session, Simone complained of feeling shaky and tearful. The previous day, her boss, Roberta, snapped at her.

"But didn't your laboratory just lose its research grant funding for next year in the Bernie Madoff scandal, and aren't you now applying for

Federal grant funding to replace it?" I asked. "And do you think you both might be feeling a lot of pressure and experiencing anxiety and stress?"

Simone agreed that I had a good point. We did one round of NBD on the shock of being snapped at. Simone realized both she and Roberta knew how to do NBD, but neither of them thought to use it because they hadn't recognized the subtle symptoms of trauma.

Later that day, Roberta came to apologize for snapping at Simone. Simone suggested they use a code word as a special signal to remind each other to do NBD when they noticed signs of stress in each other. In her next coaching session, Simone reported to me that the plan was working well, and she and Roberta were both feeling and working together much better.

TRAUMA CAN CAUSE SLEEPLESSNESS

Janine

Janine, a hardworking software engineer in her fifties, avoided looking at her retirement and investment account statements because she knew the numbers would be down, and she didn't want to upset herself. She figured she still had her job, she wasn't planning to retire anytime soon, she couldn't figure out any place else to put her money, and if she did transfer her money now, she wouldn't recoup her losses when the market bounced back. *Surely the market will recover in about 20 years when I need the money*, she thought.

Tax time rolled around, and Janine had to look at her financial statements. Inexplicably, she woke up at 3:00 a.m. and couldn't get back to sleep. Janine called me. We discovered that Janine expected the value of her accounts to be down by half, but was shocked to discover they were *down by two-thirds*. In that instant, her unconscious mind imagined her getting old with no income and living in misery at a dingy welfare retirement home. One round of the NBD technique cleared her phobic reaction and corrected her sleeplessness.

Larry

Larry, CEO of a multi-million-dollar business training and executive coaching company, had to lay off 20% of his employees due to a drop in annual revenues. He tried not to think about the effect this would have on those employees who had, in fact, done their jobs well. He tried not to think about the negative effect this would have on the remaining staff's morale. He tried not to think about how he would have to take a cut in pay because his salary was tied to the company's income. He tried not to admit he felt like he'd failed everyone who depended on him for not bringing in the business. He refused to believe he couldn't single-handedly shield his company from the effects of the country's massive economic downturn.

But the day of the layoffs, Larry stopped sleeping. At Larry's next HBLU™ business coaching session, we treated him for all the traumatic loss he experienced, and that night, he returned to sleeping comfortably. And, as is usual when we heal patterns in the unconscious mind and body, Larry came up with some innovative ideas for moving the company forward and returned to work excited and motivated.

Ronald

Ronald, a retired businessman living off investments and a little bit of Social Security income, stopped sleeping. He had to cut way back on his and his wife's spending because their income had dropped so substantially. But that wasn't all that bothered him.

He invested in his son's now-failing business. Moreover, his son had just bought a home last year and was financially overextended. His daughter had just been laid off from her job. Ronald, accustomed to being a successful businessman father was now *unable to help his children.* He woke up in the night worrying about them.

During Ronald's HBLU™ session, we carefully listed and treated everything he was worried about. Ronald felt like he could sleep well after this and promised to use NBD if he woke up again in the middle of the night.

TRAUMA CAN MAKE IT HARD TO MAINTAIN YOUR INTEGRITY

Linda

Linda, a therapist specializing in marriage and family counseling, saw a drop in her client load for the first time in years. Normally, when she got calls from people looking for addiction counseling, she referred them to a colleague who specialized in that area. Now, she found herself considering widening her practice to treat patients who weren't her specialty. Somehow, that didn't feel right, and she continued to refer clients to those practitioners she felt would best serve them.

During her HBLU™ session, we found that the sight of empty calendar spaces triggered the fear that she'd lose her practice and be worthless. One round of NBD cleared her phobic reaction and eliminated her ethical dilemma. She realized even though she was afraid, the best way to maintain her sense of self-worth and integrity was to continue to rely on her best professional judgment.

Cheryl

Cheryl, a school psychologist at a school for severely emotionally disturbed and violent children, reported feeling unusually exhausted. Although Cheryl normally tries to please everybody, she's accustomed to handling the predictable conflicts between parents, teachers, and children in the design of an individualized behavior management and teaching plan. This time, though, the negative effects of the national and state economic downturn on school funding, and the drop in value of her retirement and other investments, made her more stressed and vulnerable to others' opinions of her. She was disturbed by disagreement from some of the staff and parents about her behavioral management plans for a couple of the students, and felt unsupported by the administration.

At her HBLU™ session, we discovered the fatigue was caused by the fear that she would get fired for doing what she was supposed to. After clearing this phobia with one round of NBD, she realized, "If I do what I know is right, the results of that action are only going to lead to more rightness. If I did get fired because the system is flawed, then I shouldn't be there. I won't give my energy away to fear. I can't control the future. I can only continue to do what's right. Doing what is right professionally is more likely to protect my job than trying not to get people angry."

Samuel

Samuel, an engineer at a software company, reported feeling anxious about attending his next staff meeting. His company had laid off several people in his department, but they still needed to deliver the latest version of the software on time. The manager of his department asked the remaining staff to volunteer to do the extra work. Samuel agreed to add an extra part of the project to his schedule, then worked through several weekends, putting a strain on his body and his marriage.

In the end, Samuel was late in delivering his own part of the project. He was afraid that by overextending himself, the quality of his own work would suffer and harm his reputation. At his HBLU™ business coaching session, we prepared Samuel for his department meeting by treating his fear (with one round of NBD) that if he said no to his manager, he'd get fired and be worthless. He realized it was better to stop volunteering and focus on the quality of his work than it was to people-please.

All my clients knew how to do the NBD technique for clearing traumatic shock before they came to these specific HBLU™ sessions, but *they hadn't thought to use it* because the shock they experienced was too subtle to recognize consciously!

So, if shock can be so subtle, how do you know when to use NBD? I recommend that during stressful times, you do it in the morning when you wake up as you think about what you dread might happen that day (i.e., more bad news at your company), and at night before bedtime, looking back over anything upsetting that happened that day. **Use NBD when you have trouble sleeping, or feel irritable, tearful, shaky, short-tempered, impatient, anxious, exhausted, or stressed.** Use NBD just in case!

During stressful economic times, it's important to manage your emotional state, particularly your fears. That way, you can keep a positive attitude, stay motivated, access your ability to be creative and resourceful, and *preserve your relationships*, all necessities for surviving in hard times.

PART 3: TRANSITION TRAUMA

Transition trauma is the trauma people experience when they go from one situation to another. It's obvious that if you're forced to leave a situation, it codes as a loss. But even in cases where you choose to go somewhere else, and the new situation is clearly better, all transitions involve loss.

I've seen many people get their dream job or find their ideal spouse, but the new circumstances involve relocating their office, their home, and more. As happily and eagerly as they're looking forward to the new, there are things that they'll miss about the old. They may miss some of their coworkers, friends, family, lovely home, garden, neighborhood, the environment or culture of their town, etc. It's important to acknowledge and treat the losses as part of the transition process.

LIFE STAGE TRANSITION TRAUMAS

"Mom!" my daughter exclaimed in her *you're irritating me* voice, "I think you traumatized when I got accepted to college."

"What?" I replied, confused. "I felt happy for you and relieved that after all the applications and waiting, you finally got accepted somewhere that you wanted to go. What makes you think I'm traumatized?"

Looking back over the last three days, I realized that I'd tried to kiss her more than usual. "Is it because I've been trying to kiss you more than usual?"

"Yes," she replied, "and it's driving me crazy!"

"All right," I said, "I'll (meridian) tap on myself and take care of it."

As children grow and leave the previous developmental stage behind, parents experience this as a loss trauma. "Johnny is not my baby/little boy/teenager anymore." The anticipatory phobia of loss causes parents to treat their children as if they're younger than they really are, and can slow their children's development. I recommend all parents clear the loss trauma they experience as their child enters each new life-stage for the sake of themselves as well as their children.

One of the classic examples of life-stage transition trauma occurs when children actually leave home to start their adult lives. Some may leave to go to college, the military, marriage, or work, but when they leave, both the parents and the children experience a loss. I chronicled my husband's and my experience of my daughter's leaving for college in my newsletter below.

COLLEGE TRANSITION TRAUMA CAUSES EMPTY NEST SYNDROME

COLLEGE BOUND PART I

I wake up too early feeling sad. My only child is going to college next week. As I process the loss, I realize I'm losing *the center of my life*.

Knowing she's leaving, I've been trying to prepare by thinking about all the things I wanted to do but didn't because I had to be home for her. I could go back to evening yoga and aerobics classes. I could finish writing my books. My husband and I could get theater subscriptions. We could have friends again! While getting excited about getting my own life back, I realized I was carefully avoiding picturing her empty room. I pictured coping by leaving her door closed the entire time she's away.

But I have no other choice. I have to launch her properly. So, I treated myself with the HBLU™ protocol for clearing trauma. In addition, whenever I felt triggered by environmental cues—i.e., the road to the high school we'd never be driving to again, or the store in the mall where we used to shop, but she's now outgrown—I did the NBD (meridian tapping) technique to clear the traumatic reaction.

Meanwhile, my husband talks about how happy and relieved he is that she's leaving soon, that the labor-intensive process of getting her into and out to college will soon be over, and how I can have my car back. My daughter talks about how excited she is to go to college, and how she can't wait to get away from us. *Am I the only one who feels sad?* I wondered. I realized I carried their sadness for them. Isn't that just typical that the wife/mother carries all the emotion for the whole family? Three minutes of boundary tapping took care of that. *Process your own damn sadness*, I thought.

I'm grateful that I have HBLU™ tools to help me through the process. Reaching out to other parents who are going through or have gone through the same thing also gives me some comfort.

So, I still can't quite believe she's going to be gone, and I feel sad and lonely when I think about it. But now I'm sleeping through the night.

COLLEGE BOUND PART II

My husband and I took my daughter to college and made sure her room felt like home. We discussed the fact that, as an adult, we expect her to remain connected with us by regularly sharing what's going on in her life. We reminded her, "We're connected forever as a family, no matter where we live. And furthermore, our home is still your permanent address, and your bedroom is your bedroom until you get a job and rent your own apartment." She nodded at that and stopped asking us if we were happy to be getting rid of her.

The next day, my husband and I went to all the orientation seminars. I cried a lot, but felt reassured that the school would take good care of my daughter. My daughter wouldn't sit anywhere near us and wouldn't go with us to any of the other activities. She couldn't wait for us to leave. So later that day, we exchanged brief hugs and left.

On the drive home, we decided to visit Howe Caverns, an underground cavern with stalactites and stalagmites in Upstate New York. There were many families with young children on the tour, and I started to feel sad. I realized I felt old because we didn't have any children living at home with us anymore. One round of tapping cleared that feeling with the learning that you're never old, as long as you're still active. I also had to treat environmental triggers such as buying much less food at the grocery store (because now there are only two of us) and what to do with ourselves on the weekends, since our lives no longer revolve around her activities.

I've treated several other mothers for college transition trauma, and they all had the same reactions. A couple of mothers raised in abusive and alcoholic, dysfunctional families also feared their daughters would cut them off completely in the same way they cut off their own mothers as soon as they could get away from them. One round of tapping took care of this phobia. These mothers happily realized they'd been very different and much better mothers to their children than their own mothers had been, and took pride in breaking the pattern of family dysfunction.

I'm slowly getting used to spending time with my husband in the evenings, and talking, Skyping, and texting my daughter. People who've gone through it tell me I'll soon be enjoying the freedom.

COLLEGE BOUND PART III

We're adjusting. Not surprisingly, my daughter is self-sufficient and happy with her college and getting good grades.

My husband was another matter. Accustomed to planning and making things happen for her, he bought tickets for her and six of her friends to attend a hockey game here in Boston. He was grappling with the logistics of transporting the group when my daughter phoned. "We got season tickets to all the home games, which will make it easy to see games!" He angrily asked, "So that means you won't be coming to Boston?" My daughter quickly hung up.

I asked him, "What is this? All the energy just drained out of the room. Is this how you cope with feeling disappointed or unappreciated?"

"Let me work on it," he said.

The next day, he reported that he realized he was no longer the high school daddy responsible for making her life happen according to her wishes. "She's in college now, and I can't make any plans for her anymore." He said he treated himself with HBLU™ to adjust to his new role of college daddy who just pays the tuition bills.

The next day was Saturday, and he woke up so dizzy that he stayed in bed all day. "Do you think this is a trauma from having lost your role as do-everything-for-her Daddy?" I asked. "No, I think it's a virus," he said.

But as it turned out, it was a **disorientation trauma**, in which the loss of his role and his sense of purpose (i.e., the center of his life) was so disorienting, it made him dizzy. To get back his sense of balance, we had to clear not only the emotional disorientation reaction, but all the physical disorientation traumas he'd ever experienced, including the childhood ear infections and accompanying motion sickness, roller coaster rides, falling while skiing, and being hit in the head with a baseball during Little League practice.

The following week, a client who's a single mother came in complaining of dizziness. Her son, the last child at home, had just gone to college and was doing well. "I'll bet I know what this is," I said.

Her son got into trouble with drugs and alcohol and barely graduated from high school. At an unconscious level, a part of her expected him to fail. So, at the conscious level, she was relieved he was doing well at college. But when he told her he was probably getting all A's in his classes, she unconsciously realized he wouldn't be coming home, and he didn't need a mother to take care of him in that way anymore. She was so disoriented that she immediately became dizzy. HBLU™ treatment for the **disorientation trauma** cleared up her symptoms.

As for me, after treating myself with the NBD technique for the feeling of missing my daughter, I could finally watch another episode of last summer's TV series "So You Think You Can Dance." And miraculously, the weather was going to be 80 degrees that weekend! So, we bought an automated cat feeder and went to Cape Cod.

PART 4: NEAR-DEATH EXPERIENCES

If someone has a severe physical injury trauma from an accident, surgery, or illness, they may have had a near-death experience. I've seen people who had near-death experiences from car and motorcycle accidents, surgical procedures for bleeding ulcers, ruptured aneurysms, heart attacks, and even a C-section. One person had a near-death experience during a thyroid storm (a sudden and intense surge of thyroid hormones that can be fatal).

Some people remember a near-death experience consciously as an experience of floating above their body, looking down on the scene. Some remember getting as far as going through a tunnel of light and meeting previously deceased relatives, angelic beings, Jesus, or even God. Others have no conscious recollection of a near-death experience.

This trauma should be treated by a healing professional who can do muscle testing since the person may or may not remember the experience consciously. That's why it's important to muscle test and ask their deepest wisdom if they had a near-death experience during any severe physical injury traumas or illnesses for which they're being treated. If the person did have a near-death experience, the fact that they're alive and talking indicates it wasn't their time to die, and the soul returned to the body.

When a person has a near-death experience, the soul's leaving and coming back into the body is not *physically* traumatic. The *body* imprints an *emotional* loss trauma, with the highest priority emotion being shame that the body didn't do its job well enough to be a good host for the soul.

To treat a near-death experience, start by treating any physical injury trauma. Then treat the body for the emotional loss trauma of losing the soul.

PART 5: SEPARATION ANXIETY

Separation anxiety is caused by a subtle loss trauma in children under age three. I found this out by accident when I went to a four-day training when my daughter, Laura, was 18 months old. I made it a point to talk with her every night by phone and kiss each other goodnight. On my first day back, I put on my coat to go to work. Laura ran up and said, "Mommy, don't go, you'll get lost."

Puzzled, I replied, "Laura, I'm just going to work, and I'll be home this evening. I only work five minutes from home, and you've been to my office and know where it is. I won't get lost."

Later that day, I called our colleague, Helen Tuggy, Ph.D. (a clinical psychologist whom I consider to be a walking encyclopedia of psychology). After telling her the story, I asked, "Helen, do you think Laura could have a loss trauma from me going away?"

Helen explained that object relations theory defines object permanence to be the ability to know that something exists even if it's out of sight. Psychological research demonstrated that in the early months of life, if you show a baby a rattle, it will smile and reach for it, but if you move the rattle out of sight, the baby does not move its head to follow or look for it. It just thinks it's gone. The ability to know an object exists even when it's out of sight develops at about nine months old. The child continues to be able to remember the object's existence for longer and longer periods of time up to the age of three. Before that, if a parent is gone from a child for more than 24 hours, the child concludes that the parent is dead and imprints a loss trauma.

I went home, started rocking Laura on my lap in the rocking chair, and said, "Remember when Mommy went away last week and didn't come home for a few days and you thought I was dead?" I started treating her with the NBD technique and continued the story. "I'm not dead, and I am home now and everything is fine." I finished tapping her through the entire tapping sequence, and Laura never mentioned it again.

Knowing this now, I recommend that my clients not leave their children for a whole day until after they're three years old. If they're taking a vacation, going on a business trip, or attending some important family function where they can't bring children, and even if they leave the children with parents or close relatives, I recommend they treat their children for separation trauma with NBD as soon as they get back.

PART 6: BIRTH TRAUMA

Birth is a very physically and emotionally demanding process for both the mother and the baby. Babies get squeezed and pulled. If labor is too long, the baby will be born with claustrophobia. Imagine being in a baby's body.

Babies come from a warm, dark, and quiet environment to an environment that can be shocking to the senses. Their wet bodies hit cold air and experience bright lights, loud noises, and sudden movements. This can cause sensory processing disorder. After birth, the umbilical cord is supposed to be cut when it stops pulsing. If the cord is wrapped around the neck or is cut too soon, the baby may have suffocation trauma.

The baby may be swaddled too tightly in a blanket, causing restraint trauma, or whisked off to a nursery too quickly, causing neglect or attachment trauma. They may be drugged from anesthesia given to their mothers, or worse, drugs from the mother's addictions. And if the mother was completely asleep, the child may think their mother is dead and they killed her.

For the mother, giving birth can result in trauma from labor pains, loss of blood, feelings of violation if she has a history of sexual abuse, physical injury to the abdominal muscles from long labor or Caesarian section, and trauma to the bladder. Most trauma to the mother resolves spontaneously when the baby is handed to her and laid on her chest, resulting in a surge of oxytocin, which neutralizes the fight or flight reaction. Depending on circumstances, there might be remaining trauma to the body or emotional trauma that prevents bonding.

Fortunately, birth trauma can be cleared using the NBD technique.

Car Seat Trauma

Infants don't have much rational conscious awareness or language skills. Thus, you must physically elicit the phobic reaction to clear it. For example, children with claustrophobia from birth trauma often scream when they're buckled into their car seats. To clear this, put the child in the car seat and perform NBD.

I also found car seat trauma in a baby adopted from China. Her adoptive parents reported that she would scream inconsolably when put in a car seat, and it was worse at night. Further investigation revealed this child was found in a basket in front of a grocery store in China. She was probably driven there in some kind of car seat in the middle of the night. I recommended her adoptive parents put her in a car seat at night and treat her with NBD while making comforting comments about how she is safe and wanted. It worked for this child and for several other babies adopted from China.

Laura

During birth, my daughter Laura got stuck coming out and had to be helped with vacuum suction that left a couple of scabs on her head. Five weeks later, my husband realized that every time he pulled a T-shirt over Laura's head, she screamed. He concluded it was birth trauma. So, we put Laura on the changing table, pulled a T-shirt over her head, and when she screamed on cue, we tapped on her. She stopped screaming and never reacted to a T-shirt again.

Edith

For as long as she could remember, Edith's right leg would twist and spasm uncontrollably every time she lay down to sleep. She tried everything to get it to stop spasming, including muscle relaxants, medication for restless leg syndrome, chiropractic treatment, acupuncture, magnesium, and other minerals to no avail. During her HBLU™ session, we discovered the leg spasms were caused by birth trauma.

Edith was born face down, and the doctor turned her over to suction her too quickly while her feet were still in the vagina, causing her legs to twist. Lying down triggered the twist memory. We did two rounds of NBD. During the first round, she visualized being turned over and focused on the twist sensation. In the second round, she ran the scene backward to undo the twist as if it had never happened. That night, for the first time in her life, she had no leg spasms. Two days later, she reported she had no leg spasms. A year later, the leg spasms were still gone.

These were a couple of simple examples of treating birth trauma. But birth trauma has many possible layers. If you suspect you have birth trauma, I recommend you work with a professional trained in HBLU™, energy psychology, rebirthing, or body-centered psychotherapy.

CHAPTER 5

PHYSICAL INJURY TRAUMA

Most people recognize that physical blows to the body caused by car accidents, physical fights, sports injuries, and certain sudden internal injuries from heart attacks and strokes cause injury to the body. There are many other, more subtle, but just as powerful causes of physical injury to the body, and it's important to recognize these traumas and treat them. In this chapter, in addition to the aforementioned types of injuries, I describe physical injuries to various parts of the body, including the brain from illness, surgery, drugs and alcohol, and other more obscure causes.

PART 1: DIRECT PHYSICAL BLOWS

As a reminder, a phobic reaction is a conditioned response of the fight/flight/freeze reflex that starts when a person experiences a traumatic shock (physical or emotional). At the time the flight/fight/freeze reflex fired off, anything in the environment could get associated with that memory. Later on, these associations can trigger this original reflex reaction (like a body flashback), resulting in a phobic reaction, even when nothing dangerous or upsetting occurs in the present moment.

When a body experiences physical trauma from injury or illness, it holds the trauma memory in the tissues, and when something in the environment triggers those memories, the body reacts with physical symptoms.

I have found that energy psychology techniques are very effective treatments for clearing physical injury trauma from the body.

I've treated many people for chronic pain or other symptoms of illnesses caused by physical injury trauma. I found that energy psychology techniques work most efficiently and completely to release trauma memory and its resulting symptoms from the body. Natural Bio-Destressing (NBD) is a good all-purpose technique for releasing the memory of physical injury in the body.

Trauma remains imprinted in the body forever unless specifically removed by an appropriate energy psychology technique.

My 93-year-old grandmother, who moved to assisted living the previous year, complained of back pain. Perhaps it was caused by her relative immobility; she now lived in one room and had trouble walking because of chronic bursitis in her knees. Perhaps it was a problem with her hospital bed mattress.

I muscle tested her to determine the source of her pain and was surprised to discover it was from a car accident at age 16! She recounted to me in vivid detail that as a front-seat passenger, she was hurled into the dashboard when the driver rear-ended the car in front of them. They didn't have seatbelts in those days. She wrenched her back and also hurt her knees. Several rounds of NBD cleared the physical and emotional trauma, and the back pain went away. I took this as direct evidence that trauma remains trapped in the body forever (or at least for 77 years) unless it is specifically removed using appropriate techniques.

Clearing the anticipatory phobias in physical injury traumas is the key to clearing chronic pain and recovering physical function.

Physical anticipatory phobias manifest as tightness or protective holding back on fully using a formerly injured part of the body. It can result in pain in the area that was directly injured, or it may be in another part of the body that's trying to compensate for the injury. Clearing the physical anticipatory phobia is the key step to reconstituting full function of that area of the body. Limping disappears, improved or full range of motion is restored, and pain disappears. I tell my clients that we won't know how much of their pain is from trauma and how much of it is purely physical until we clear the trauma. After the trauma is cleared, I typically see the pain drop by a minimum of 50% to a maximum of 100%. Any remaining pain needs physical treatment of some sort.

John

During an American Humanistic Psychology conference, I demonstrated clearing physical injury trauma on John, a man who fell off a ladder while painting the back of his house five years earlier. He broke both his right shoulder and his right leg. Since there was nobody home at the time, he had to crawl from the back yard to the front yard so somebody would find and help him. John fainted several times from the pain, but eventually made it to the front yard, and a neighbor rescued him. He had surgery to repair the broken bone in his leg, but he still limped noticeably. His shoulder motion was impaired such that he couldn't reach above and behind him for a football throw.

John's deepest wisdom said we could clear the emotional and physical trauma at the same time. At the moment he first lost his balance, John felt he had lost his life and his marriage. The first intervention cleared the shock, fear, and anger. We did two interventions on sadness; the first round was the sadness about losing his life, and the second round was the sadness he felt when he imagined his wife finding him dead in the backyard. Two more rounds of treatment cleared the rest of the loss outline up to the anticipatory phobia.

The emotional anticipatory phobia was the fear that he could fall off a ladder again. A physical anticipatory phobia expresses itself as a protective stiffness, shielding, or hesitation to move that the body uses to prevent re-injury. In this case, the physical anticipatory phobias were in the hip muscles of the right leg, causing his limp, and in the right shoulder blade, preventing full range of motion of his arm. One more intervention cleared all the anticipatory phobias. John instantly regained full use of his football-throwing arm and walked out of the room without a limp!

Sarah

Sarah was a 60-plus-year-old woman who fell down three steps in her backyard, breaking her ankle. The ankle healed, but six months later, she developed a mysterious pain in her hip. After six months of medical treatment and physical therapy, the hip remained the same. When she came to me for treatment, we discovered she had two distinct physical injury traumas that we had to treat separately.

The first trauma was in the ankle, but the second trauma was in the knee that twisted around as she fell. The physical anticipatory phobia for both traumas was located in the hip, which was trying to remain stiff to prevent twisting and falling. Six months after clearing these physical injury traumas, Sarah called to report that the hip pain had "mysteriously" cleared up a couple of months after treatment.

Fred

Fred was a 40-something man with a passion for motorcycles. Seven years earlier, he was hit by a car while driving his motorcycle and was very badly injured. He died three times on the operating table and eventually lost his left foot, which was crushed beyond repair. After surgery, his wife at the time brought his two children to his hospital room. "Say goodbye to your father, girls," she told them.

Fred divorced his wife and remarried. He wore a foot prosthesis, but never wore shorts, never ran, and never danced. Fred had chronic pain and slept in a waterbed because he was never comfortable lying down. He always sat with one leg stiffly extended off the side of a chair.

Fred had several physical and emotional losses tied to this one event, and we methodically cleared them all. To his wife's amazement, when we were done, Fred ran down two flights of stairs and sat down normally in a chair. His pain was gone, and he regained range of motion in his leg. I recommended he get fitted for a new prosthesis that would support his new posture.

Six months later, Fred's left hip developed a painful case of bursitis. Fred's astonished doctor told him, "The bursitis was caused by the instant reconstitution of function." It was as if his leg had been in a cast for seven years, his muscles had atrophied, and when the cast came off, he was suddenly using muscles he hadn't used in years. I recommended Fred treat his body as if he'd just had a cast removed, and go for physical therapy and acupuncture. Fred decided to tough it out, figuring the leg would recover by itself, and it did.

Jane

Jane was an Olympic skier. Ten days prior to the Olympics, she had a skiing accident in which her ski cut through her left calf to the bone. The accident severed the nerve to her leg, preventing any feeling below the knee. She got her injury stitched up and skied the Olympics on one leg. She didn't do well in her race.

Five years later, Jane's lower leg was still numb. While clearing the physical injury trauma, she reported a feeling like lightning going down her leg. She immediately regained 75% sensation in her leg. Although she was now somewhat older than her competitors, she returned to skiing, won two world championships, and missed qualifying for the next Olympics by one point.

Treatment for Physical Injury Trauma

When I treat people to clear physical injury trauma from physical causes such as accidents and surgery, I look with a microscopic eye at what's going on in the body (think like a body, meaning pretend to be that body part).

For example, if someone had breast cancer and had a breast or part of their breast removed, from the body's point of view, it lost something. In this case, it lost breast tissue. Bodies really don't like to lose parts of themselves.

Check for emotional trauma from cancer (clear diagnosis shock), but also check for physical injury from the cancer itself, surgery, chemotherapy, and radiation. Consider all remaining physical symptoms, such as trouble raising their arm due to pulling around the scar, lymphedema, neuropathy, and physical injury to the digestive system, skin, and hair follicles. Emotionally, if tissue was removed, ask what that tissue represented and whether they feel they lost their attractiveness, femininity, youth, etc.

While checking the tissues involved in breast surgery, ask if there's physical injury trauma to the skin, muscles underneath the skin, the fascia (the onion skin, stretchy layer of Saran Wrap-like tissue that holds things in place), breast tissue, lymph nodes, blood vessels, nerves, fat cells, and ribs. Dissect layers of tissue in your mind and ask if there is trauma. Interestingly, residual pain from physical injury trauma is held in the fascia, not so much in the nerves.

If someone slipped on black ice, fell on their shoulder, dislocated or tore a rotator cuff, and then had surgery, check for physical injury trauma to the bones, including the collarbone, where it attaches to the shoulder socket, or the shoulder bone, where it attaches to the collarbone socket. Is there any physical injury trauma to the tendons, ligaments, muscles, cartilage, bursa, blood vessels, nerves, or fascia? If they had surgery on top of it, check for physical injury trauma to the skin as well as the regular tissues, blood vessels, nerves, fascia, muscles, tendons, ligaments, cartilage, bursa, or the bone itself.

As you can see from these examples, physical injury trauma leaves lingering physical symptoms even though the tissue has healed. Clearing the remaining trauma imprint from the body is key to eliminating the remaining symptoms and recovering as much function as possible.

PART 2: ILLNESSES CAN CAUSE PHYSICAL INJURY

When I think about physical injury, I used to think about car accidents, sports injuries, and other situations involving a physical impact to your body. Then I discovered people can have physical injury traumas from illnesses, drugs, foods, and infections!

Physical Injury from Respiratory Infections Causing Pneumonia

Lillian

Lillian came to my office looking pale and gray. "I have pneumonia, and I'm upset because I feel too sick to attend an important meeting this evening," she reported. A few days earlier, Lillian was bitten by a dog when she volunteered at the animal shelter, and her coworkers recommended she get a tetanus shot.

Although Lillian insisted all she needed was a tetanus vaccine, the doctor only had the DPT (diphtheria, pertussis, tetanus) vaccine in stock, so he gave her that. Two days later, she had pneumonia, which was verified on X-ray. Her doctor prescribed the antibiotic used for diphtheria. Since the diphtheria vaccine only contains inactivated diphtheria toxoid, acellular pertussis antigens, and inactivated tetanus toxin, it wasn't possible for her to get any kind of infection from the vaccine.

Muscle testing revealed the vaccine triggered a body flashback to the trauma memory of an actual diphtheria infection at age two! We did the HBLU™ protocol for clearing physical injury to the body, and by the end of the session, her color and energy returned to normal, and her symptoms cleared up. She happily attended her meeting that evening and told everybody I had "cured" her of pneumonia.

Any kind of illness can leave physical injury trauma in the body. Bronchial infections, pneumonia, sinus infections, and ear infections at any time in your life leave physical injury trauma memory in the tissues. People who had a severe respiratory infection in childhood often notice that what causes mild cold symptoms in others causes worse symptoms in them. Everyone else gets a mild runny nose from a cold that's going around, but invariably, people with physical injury trauma experience the cold going right to their lungs. This is because as soon as the body notices it's starting to get sick, it says, "Oh, no. Not another ___ (flashback to the traumatic infection)," and recreates the symptoms of the original infection.

When I treat people to clear physical injury trauma to the lungs and respiratory system from infections, or other causes such as smoking or exposure to chemicals or cold air, I look with a microscopic eye at what's going on in the body and check for physical injury trauma to the:

1. Lungs, bronchi, alveoli, pleura around the lungs, larynx, and trachea
2. Tonsils, mouth, tissues of the throat, and eustachian tubes of the ears
3. Sinuses, head

4. Ribs, chest muscles, and back from coughing
5. Stomach or esophagus, and the diaphragm from coughing
6. Other internal organs
7. Whole body from fever or bacterial toxins

Of course, the best thing to do is to stay healthy. A healthy diet, exercise, sleep, nutrition, and supplements to support optimum body function, and minimum exposure to toxins such as smoke, alcohol, and recreational drugs are obvious ways to do so. Since trauma suppresses the immune system, I also recommend tapping for anything that upsets you.

Physical Injury from Respiratory Infections Causing Asthma

Linda

Linda had asthma. She ended up in the hospital every time she caught a cold. Muscle testing revealed that her lungs were traumatized from an episode of severe bronchitis at age two and an episode of pneumonia at age five. The body had physical injury trauma due to irritation from the viral infections, the high fever, and the coughing.

Every time Linda began to get symptoms of a cold, her body and unconscious mind flashed back to the memory of the original infection, triggering a reaction of, "Oh no, not bronchitis again!" and physically generated bronchitis-like symptoms in the form of asthma. Clearing these physical injury traumas eliminated any further asthma symptoms.

Physical Injury from Gastrointestinal Infections

We've seen several cases of intestinal trauma, which caused a range of problems, including hemorrhoid flare-ups, urination problems, interstitial cystitis, and vaginal infections. Several individuals undergoing a colonoscopy experienced intestinal trauma from the medication used to clean out the intestines before the test, and from the physical irritation of the procedure itself. Several individuals experienced intestinal trauma due to antibiotic treatment that kills the normal protective bacteria in the gut and vagina. Another person experienced intestinal trauma after eating an authentic and extremely spicy preparation of Thai food. Common intestinal infections that cause physical injury trauma to the gut include viruses that cause intestinal flu, bacteria such as *Salmonella*, *E. coli*, and *Campylobacter*, and parasites such as *Giardia lamblia*, *Cryptosporidium parvum*, and *Entamoeba histolytica*. I've also seen physical injury trauma to the gut cause food allergies or sensitivities, including lactose intolerance, that were reversed after treatment.

I highly recommend that you do an inventory of your life from your body's point of view and treat any physical injury traumas from drugs, food, or infections. You'll feel *much* better.

PART 3: PHYSICAL INJURY FROM SURGERY

Sam

Sam needed a quadruple bypass operation. We performed the surgery preparation protocol to prevent his body from traumatizing, and concentrated on preparing his chest wall, ribs, and heart to perceive and cooperate with the surgery as a healing intervention. After surgery, his lungs filled with so much fluid that he had trouble breathing when lying down.

It was so uncomfortable, he had trouble sleeping. The fluid had to be drained three times. His doctors said these postoperative symptoms were normal, but I didn't believe that. I told Sam, "Although fluid buildup is common, that doesn't make it normal."

Upon muscle testing, we discovered his lungs imprinted a trauma at the moment the doctors stopped his breathing to put him on the heart-lung machine. From the lungs' point of view, the only time breathing stops is when you're dead. Since his lungs assumed they were dead, they didn't return to full function after the surgery, causing them to accumulate fluid. After clearing the physical injury trauma, Sam's lungs stopped accumulating fluid.

Three months later, Sam developed cellulitis, a bacterial infection deep inside his left leg where doctors had removed veins for use in the heart bypass operation. His leg had a physical injury trauma from the veins' removal, combined with a feeling of outrage that nobody asked its permission before ripping them out. We treated the trauma, thanked the leg for its gift, and informed it that it could regrow veins. Sam never got another leg infection.

We also decided to check in with all the other tissues in Sam's body to make sure we didn't miss anything. We discovered and treated physical injury trauma to the liver from detoxifying massive amounts of anesthetic.

As I discussed in the explanation of the Healing from the Body Level Up™ methodology, all levels of our being have minds of their own, and I describe how to communicate with all levels of your being (usually using muscle testing). So yes, it's important to respect and communicate with your body, and it will communicate back with you. I go into more detail about this in the Surgery Preparation Protocol in Chapter 8.

PART 4: PHYSICAL INJURY CAUSED BY DRUGS/ MEDICATION

Interstitial Cystitis Caused by Antibiotics

Around age 45, I got interstitial cystitis. Cystitis is an inflammation of the bladder, usually caused by an E. coli bacterial infection of the bladder or urinary tract. Treated with antibiotics, it goes away. Alternatively, interstitial cystitis is characterized by bladder pain and urinary frequency with no measurable physical cause. The pain can be so bad, and the bladder urgency can be so painful and problematic, that people actually become disabled by it.

I even had blood in the urine, though there was no bacterial infection or signs of bladder injury or cancer. The doctors said it's incurable and hoped it would just fade away within five years. So, I decided to try to cure it with HBLU™ treatment. To my surprise, muscle testing revealed that the cause of the interstitial cystitis was physical injury trauma to the intestines. You might assume it would be physical injury trauma to the bladder or urinary tract, but it was the intestines.

How did this happen? I was badly emotionally betrayed by a colleague. It shocked me so severely that I felt he had punched my lights out (i.e., punched me in the nose). Two days later, I developed a bacterial sinus infection. I'd only had one other sinus infection in my life. I treated the sinus infection with a massive amount of antibiotics.

The antibiotics wiped out my intestinal flora, causing cramps, bloating, gas, and diarrhea. They also wiped out my vaginal flora, and I got a yeast infection. After I finished the course of antibiotics and cleared up the sinus infection, I took probiotics to repopulate my gut and a suppository to clear up the vaginal yeast infection, but I was left with interstitial cystitis.

I told my urologist that through muscle testing, my body reported that interstitial cystitis was caused by physical injury trauma to the intestines. He said that made sense because in females, we have one giant muscle group (the pelvic floor muscles) holding our guts in at the bottom. That muscle sheet has three openings in it: one for the urethra, one for the vagina, and one for the anus. If there's trauma to any of those tissues or organs, it can cause that one muscle to spasm, causing all three openings to spasm.

To heal the interstitial cystitis, I started by treating the physical injury trauma to the intestines from the antibiotics. I treated the actual physical irritation from the antibiotic itself and the physical injury trauma from the loss of the bacteria. Next, I cleared the physical injury trauma to the bladder from excreting the medication, which irritated the mucus membrane of the bladder. Then, I treated every other physical injury trauma the intestines had ever experienced. These included a spicy Thai food meal that left me with cramps and diarrhea for three days, every intestinal flu I ever had in my life, all food poisoning trauma, all intestinal flu trauma, and all spicy food trauma.

I cleared all vaginal yeast infection trauma, every single physical injury trauma to all organs from the waist down, then every single physical injury trauma from the knees up, including pulling a groin muscle when I fell off my bicycle at age seven. I finished by clearing the emotional betrayal trauma.

Every one of the interstitial cystitis symptoms cleared up, and I've been symptom-free ever since. In addition, I've treated several other clients for interstitial cystitis and found by muscle testing that in each case, the main cause of the symptoms was physical injury to the intestines from antibiotic treatment. I'm happy to say, this protocol I developed for myself worked successfully for them. Although clearing physical injury trauma from antibiotics typically takes just one session, depending on how many other physical and emotional traumas are associated with this syndrome, it can take seven to eight sessions to clear up all related symptoms.

PART 5: PHYSICAL INJURY TRAUMA TO THE BRAIN

Polly

Polly was an RN working on the surgical floor of a major hospital. She loved her job and was very good a bedside nursing. Unfortunately, Polly had dyslexia and kept reversing numbers in patients' records. She repeatedly got fired for patient endangerment and ended up working less and less desirable jobs. We treated Polly for the goal of healing dyslexia, and discovered it was not genetic, but rather was caused by physical injury trauma to the brain from a high fever at age eight.

We cleared the physical injury trauma, and at the end of that session, the dyslexia was corrected. A week later, Polly confirmed that she had made no numerical errors. Six months later, she reported getting a better job. One year later, Polly was happy to report that she was hired for an even better job.

Ralph

During an HBLU™ training, Ralph complained that the room was too warm. He was flushed and sweating, even though everyone else was cold; we were all wearing jackets and sweaters! For the sake of the entire class's comfort, I treated Ralph for his temperature regulation problem.

In his youth, Ralph was in the Army and did his basic training in Texas, where he was required to run long distances without water at temperatures greater than 100°F. Ralph developed heat stroke and incurred a physical injury to the part of the brain that regulates body temperature. A room temperature above 67°F triggered symptoms of heatstroke. We cleared physical injury trauma from the brain, and everyone, including Ralph, was comfortable at a room temperature of 73°F for the next four days.

Physical injury trauma to the brain can be healed

Over the years, I've treated many people for learning disabilities, ADD, faulty memory, poor concentration (brain fog), obsessive-compulsive disorders, some types of addictions, and a laundry list of difficult-to-treat symptoms that turned out to be caused by undiagnosed—but easily treatable with HBLU™—physical injury trauma to the brain.

I'm fond of saying, "The brain does many things," and there are many subtle (and not-so-subtle) causes of brain injury. Here are some of the typical symptoms my colleagues and I have successfully treated with HBLU™ since making this discovery:

Typical Brain Injury Symptoms

1. Addictions
2. Obsessive-compulsive behaviors
3. Poor memory of written or oral material
4. Reversing or misreading letters, syllables, or even whole words
5. Difficulty doing math
6. Difficulty remembering melodies or words to songs
7. Inability to organize or prioritize paperwork or other important life details
8. Brain fog or forgetfulness
9. Difficulty focusing or unfocusing attention
10. Difficulty processing certain types of emotional stress
11. Physical symptoms such as dizziness, lack of coordination, headaches
12. Inability to feel full, even though the person has eaten enough
13. Inability to regulate body temperature
14. Dysregulated breathing

People with impaired brain function know their brains aren't working right, and they feel anxious, stupid, incompetent, worthless, and often unlovable. They work hard to compensate for the deficiency so that it hardly shows. Meanwhile, their friends, relatives, and teachers accuse them of being lazy, resistant, or passive-aggressive. This leaves them feeling humiliated and traumatized.

Alternatively, their friends, relatives, and teachers all assure them they're intelligent and talented, and are pretending to make up a problem where, based on results, none exists. Rather than feeling supported, the person with impaired brain function feels misunderstood and isolated. Only people who have this problem know what it's like to try to use an area of the brain that doesn't work. The brain itself ***experiences an anxiety reaction that exacerbates the physical malfunction, creating a vicious cycle.*** Thankfully, brain function can now be restored partially or completely by using the HBLU™ protocol for clearing physical injury trauma.

I have found that physical injury trauma to the brain comes from a number of common and not-so-common experiences.

Brain Injury Causes

1. Physical blows to the head, particularly those severe enough to cause unconsciousness or concussions.
2. Physical interventions to the brain, including surgery and electroshock therapy.
3. High fevers, particularly the kind that cause hallucinations.
4. Drugs, especially hallucinogens and psychoactive prescription medication.
5. General anesthetic.
6. Lack of oxygen caused by birth trauma, drowning, open-heart surgery, and other near-death experiences.
7. Strokes.
8. Detoxing.
9. Disease and infections (including encephalitis, viral infections including herpes, COVID, multiple sclerosis, and others).
10. Low blood sugar.

To heal physical injury trauma to the brain, muscle test through the list of symptoms, then through the list of causes. Muscle test to determine the priority physical injury cause and treat it using the standard trauma outline and the NBD technique. Treating the physical injury traumas unblocks the disabled brain pathways and allows them to function. Adding a hands-on energy transmission technique is a nice finishing step for completely "turning on" these previously dormant brain pathways. In my experience, Reiki energy does not turn on brain pathways, but other energy transmission frequencies, such as pranic healing and Shaktipath (the type of energy transmitted by Indian Gurus), work well.

Not only does clearing physical injury trauma to the brain restore normal brain functioning, but it also reverses the vicious emotional cycles the disorders created and allows the individual to feel emotionally free. People with restored brain function feel a sense of well-being, competence, and confidence that they were missing since their traumatic injury.

Testimonial #1: By L.H., Canada

On November 1, 2003, I met with Judith for a "healing brain" session. The day before, I attended Judith's presentation, "Cure Learning Disabilities and Other Brain Dysfunctions with HBLU™" at the Fifth Energy Psychology Conference in Toronto. Watching her carefully work with a patient, I realized I also had symptoms of brain injury that needed to be healed, mainly to clear long-time high-pitched squeal (tinnitus), upper- and mid-skull fogginess, and pressure in the back of my head above my neckline.

I first became a client of Judith's in 1995 when she treated me for a loss trauma, and received instant relief in one session. Since then, I have taken her courses in HBLU™, NLP, and Limiting Identities. Judith's unique research and her teachings have had an impact on me. As I have learned much about myself, I have shared my limited knowledge with others to help them. However, the above brain and head symptoms remained in the background for a number of years. Within the past year, the symptoms became much more noticeable. My chiropractor did adjustments and stated that my scalp muscles were tense, and my lower head area was more rigid than normal. So, when I saw what Judith could do in this area, I said, "Fix my head."

Several head injuries contributed to my problem. One was a head-on collision with an oncoming lumber truck. The result was stitches for the lower face area. Another time, somebody accidentally dropped a solid 80-pound bag of cement on the top of my head from a 15-foot height. The third damage to my head was in the Canadian far north, Hudson Bay, where I was delivering college courses to the Cree people. The -45°F temperatures hurt my ears even though I bundled up each time. Through each of these accidents, I felt my angels kept and guarded me, but my cellular memories retained these traumas. The beauty of Judith's work is that it recognizes and heals all levels of a person.

During the session, we cleared my fear of looking at disagreeable memories and the belief that life should be filled with only pleasant things, but people and life are sometimes unpredictable and untrustworthy. Then Judith placed her two hands above the top of my head and did some psychic adjustments and readjustments. I could feel heat coming from her hands, although they were not touching my head.

When Judith finished the session, she stood back and looked at me. Smiling broadly, she said, "Look at yourself in the mirror here. You look different." It was true. Not only did I have an immediate sense of joy and safety, I had a look of competence. The high-pitched squeal was gone. My head felt congruent and focused! I felt the "child" had "matured." It was totally incredible. My life has continued to move forward since then. My career continues to evolve. And just recently, I have been accepted into a doctoral program.

Testimonial #2: By G.H., Arizona

For years, I experienced what I came to call "brain fog" in my head. It was as if I were thinking through a dense, thick fog that interfered with my ability to process information as effectively as I wanted. In addition, I felt a heaviness in the upper right side of my head. Often, the effort to concentrate and process information through this heaviness caused headaches, blurred vision, and fatigue.

While attending Dr. Judith Swack's HBLU™ I training in February 2003, it was as if she described me when she addressed the effects of brain injury trauma. It had never occurred to me that my condition could be the consequence of brain injury trauma from concussions I'd had at least twice in my life. She graciously allowed me to be part of her research on clearing brain injury trauma. Using the techniques she developed, the brain injury was cleared, and the dormant brain pathways were activated.

During the clearing process, I could feel a physical change happening inside my head. First, there was a slight burning sensation for about three minutes in the right side of the brain. Then, I experienced energy shifting inside my head that moved throughout the whole right brain. After a few more minutes, the fog began to clear; the heaviness began to lift and continued to dissolve for the next several hours. And it has not returned.

I experienced an immediate change; it felt as if I had stepped out of the dense, heavy fog in bright, clear daylight. Even after one year, the old condition has not returned. I continue to have a "clear head" and no longer experience the headaches or fatigue caused by the previous difficulty in concentration and information retention. I consider this transition as one of the miracles in my life. Thank you and bless you, Judith, in this wonderful gift of healing!

Throughout this book, I have been discussing the fight/flight/freeze reflex and the physical and emotional residue it leaves in the conscious mind, unconscious mind, and body. This next chapter gives an in-depth explanation of the neurobiology of this reaction, the opposing calming reflex, and how meridian tapping techniques directly regulate this system. You don't need to understand the science at this level of detail to treat trauma with the protocols in this book, but if you like science, enjoy this next chapter.

CHAPTER 6

THE NEUROBIOLOGY OF ENERGY PSYCHOLOGY

A BIOMEDICAL SCIENTIST'S PERSPECTIVE ON PHYSIOLOGICAL MECHANISMS UNDERLYING ENERGY PSYCHOLOGY TREATMENTS

Since Roger Callahan published his first book on the use of meridian tapping to clear phobias in 1986 (1), I've used meridian tapping techniques to treat phobias and traumas with my clients. Many of my colleagues in the healing and counseling professions were afraid to introduce this technique for fear that their clients would think it ridiculous—"How does tapping on yourself with your hands release phobias?" or "What do you mean by energy?" or "This sounds airy-fairy"—and leave their practice.

As a Ph.D. scientist with one of my majors in neurochemistry, I understood the mechanism by which this technique worked to directly regulate the nervous system, and didn't think it strange. Since most healing practitioners aren't trained in neuroscience, I first explained the neurobiology of tapping to my colleagues in a plenary address at the 2001 Conference of the Association for Comprehensive Energy Psychology (ACEP). Since then, I've presented this seminar at many conferences for healthcare and mental healthcare professionals. Many colleagues gratefully report successfully using this explanation with their clients. In fact, one of my colleagues honored me by updating and reiterating my findings (2), and others have done more research confirming the mechanisms and efficacy of energy psychology techniques (3-5).

Note: This chapter is excerpted and updated from my original plenary address.

I'm known in the energy psychology community as the originator of Healing from the Body Level Up™ (HBLU™), which follows a scientific protocol for healing the conscious mind, unconscious mind, body, and soul levels simultaneously. I developed it from my experience as a biomedical researcher and a practitioner of mind-body healing modalities.

As practitioners of energy therapies, you may have witnessed the healing that often occurs when you work with the body to heal traumas. Here, I'll share some well-researched physiological mechanisms involved in those treatments. I'll talk about the chemistry that regulates the **fight/flight/freeze reflex** (in science this is known as the **sympathetic alarm response)**, and the opposing **calming reflex** (in science this is known as the **stress relaxation response**), which is the feedback mechanism leading to (what we call in science and medicine) homeostasis. In the energy psychology field, we call it balance.

I took the body of my seminar from the classic medical physiology textbook by Guyton and Hall (6). I also used a 1992 book by George Ulett, *Beyond Yin and Yang: How Acupuncture Really Works* (7), a wonderful paper by Dr. Stefano in Brain Research Reviews (8), and my own study of allergy subjects that describes the biochemical mechanisms of why you can cure an allergy in seconds (9).

Here, I'm going to focus on trauma. Trauma imprints at the body level, the unconscious level, and distorts conscious, rational thinking ability. So, let's look at how that happens.

I teach energy psychology techniques, how to clear phobias and traumas at Newton Community Ed, the local adult community education program. Nobody has a problem with energy psychology because this is how I explain it. When I ask my students to define a phobia, they reply that it's an exaggerated, irrational reaction that you can't control mentally. I confirm that they all know what a phobic reaction is.

Then I explain that a phobia is a conditioned response. I describe Pavlov's experiments where he demonstrated that you could train a reflex. A reflex is something you do automatically, so training a reflex should be impossible, but Pavlov did it. He trained the salivation reflex in dogs. He gave the dogs food; they salivated. Then he rang a bell, gave the dogs food; they salivated. Then, with no food around, he rang the bell, and the dogs salivated. Dogs can't eat bells, but Pavlov trained their reflex so that they associated bells with food!

Since the fight/flight/freeze reflex is a reflex, *it can be trained.* A phobic reaction is a conditioned response of the fight/flight/freeze reflex that starts when a person experiences a traumatic shock (physical or emotional). At the time the flight/fight/freeze reflex fired off, anything that was in the environment could get associated with that memory and act like the bell. Later, these associations can trigger this original reflex reaction (like a body flashback), resulting in a phobic reaction, even when nothing dangerous or upsetting is occurring in the present moment. Depending on the circumstances, the shock may imprint as a phobia, or in more severe cases, a trauma.

For every "on" system in the body, there's an "off" system. When you're too hot, you sweat, and when you're too cold, you shiver to maintain a constant body temperature. In the same way, we have a **calming reflex to neutralize the fight/flight/freeze reflex**. Some of the ways we automatically activate our calming reflex are:

- Rubbing the bridge of your nose
- Massaging your temples
- Putting your hand across your forehead (the "Oi Vey" gesture), over your mouth, or over your upper chest

- Crossing your arms
- Chewing on your fingers
- Drumming your fingertips on the desk
- Wringing your hands
- Intertwining your fingers

HOW WE UNCONSCIOUSLY RELIEVE STRESS

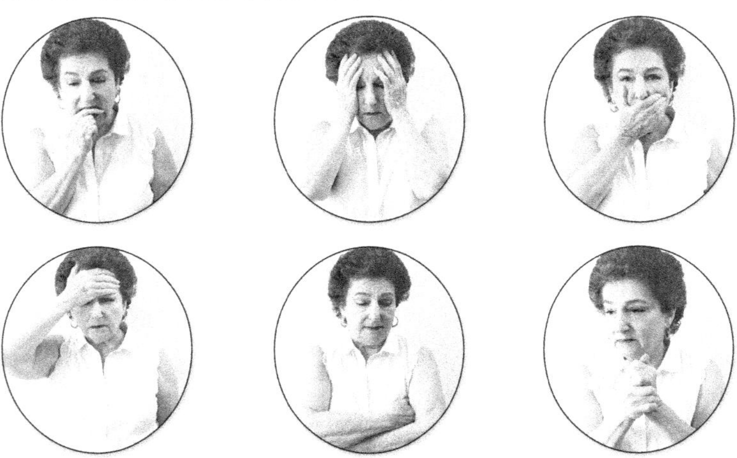

When I ask, "What do you notice when you do that?" people respond, "I feel more relaxed, I feel calmer."

"That's right," I explain. "So, you can think about what's frightening or upsetting you, and *deliberately activate all your natural stress turn-off mechanisms by tapping on these points and turning off the fight or flight reaction.* You have just *reconditioned* that experience to feel calm!

"This technique is a no-brainer because you do these behaviors all the time, every day, automatically and unconsciously. The genius here is that you can do it intentionally. You can pull up what's bothering you, you can focus on it consciously, and you can neutralize the reaction at will. That's what Natural Bio-Destressing (NBD) and meridian tapping techniques do."

The neurobiology of the fight/flight/freeze reflex (sympathetic alarm response), and the opposing calming reflex (stress relaxation response)

The Fight/Flight/Freeze Reflex

What is the function of the fight/flight/freeze reflex? Something shocks you, you get triggered, and after that, you keep flashing back and having phobic reactions. This seems really problematic, but every animal on the planet has this reflex, so it must have a positive function. But I didn't really appreciate its function until a drunk colleague told me this story at a Christmas party.

When I told him I was going to buy a new car, he told me how much he loved his motorcycle. He then launched into a very vivid description (so you know he was flashing back) of a motorcycle accident he had. A woman ran into him with her car while he was on his motorcycle. He ended up on the ground. She jumped out of the car and asked him, "Are you okay? Are you okay?"

He stood up, and being the macho kind of handsome guy he is, said, "I'm perfectly fine."

She said, "What happened to your arm?"

He said, "What do you mean?"

She was looking at the ground, so he looked at the ground. He noticed a pool of blood. He followed the trail of droplets from the ground back up into the sleeve of his leather jacket. Thankfully, he was wearing a black leather jacket.

He pulled up the sleeve and found that he'd scraped his arm very severely. He said, "Wow, look at that." Then he politely asked the woman, "Listen, my father lives about four blocks from here, so if you could do me a favor and give me a lift, he'll take me to the hospital, and I'll get this taken care of."

She exclaimed, "No problem, no problem." So, he got to the hospital, where he got it taken care of.

What's missing from this story? Pain! He had to figure out he'd scraped his arm by looking. And then I understood what this reflex is for. It numbs people to pain and gives them the strength to function long enough to save their lives!

I thought about our cavemen ancestors who also had this reflex. The wisdom teeth are starting to disappear, but we still basically have caveman bodies. As a caveman, you're part of a clan that hunts for meat. You're part of a small group of guys with spears hunting saber-tooth tigers or woolly mammoths. The likelihood you're going to get injured is pretty high. You just weren't nimble enough, you got caught by a tusk, you got gored or trampled, and boom, your fight-or-flight reflex fires off.

First of all, you go numb so you don't get overwhelmed by pain, and you can think. Second of all, you go white. All the blood drains out of your skin to the interior of your body, so you don't bleed to death through your wounds. Thirdly, your heart rate pumps up like crazy, and your muscles get really strong because you've got to crawl back to the cave before you bleed to death or are overwhelmed and paralyzed with pain. There, the medicine woman can stuff your wound with moss (like cotton to stop the bleeding) and fungus (for its antibiotic properties).

So, the purpose of this reflex is to save your life. It also shuts down your immune system and turns off your digestive system. But you don't need an immune system if you bleed to death, and you can go for a few days without food if you don't die first. Basically, all the nonessential systems get shut down, and everything gets shunted to "save my life."

Strangely enough, that same reflex fires off when a person experiences an emotional trauma. A colleague of mine's husband sat down for breakfast one day and announced that he was leaving her tomorrow for the woman he carpools with. No woolly mammoth here, but same reaction. It's still a little puzzling to me that there's not a great distinction between physical life and death and metaphorical life and death, but it's the same reflex.

Here's a diagram of the fight/flight/freeze reflex. (Figure 1)

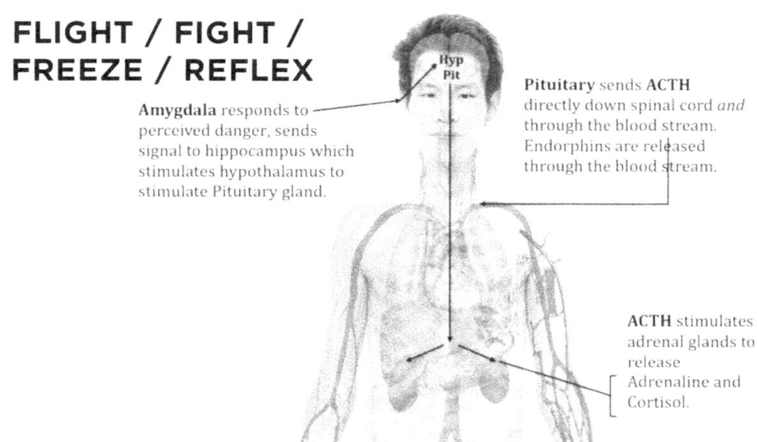

Activation of the fight/flight/freeze reflex (sympathetic alarm response) is triggered by sensory information, sending a danger signal to the amygdala. The amygdala evaluates the degree of danger by taking information from what's happening right now in the moment, as well as the information that you've stored in memory through the limbic system. This is probably where the conditioning occurs.

The fight/flight/freeze reflex can also be triggered by stress and strong emotional reactions, including from stored memories.

Then the amygdala sends a signal to the hippocampus and thalamus. The amygdala directly innervates the thalamus, and the speed of this signal is faster than the speed of information to the cerebral cortex. In fact, the length of the nerves to the alarm response is shorter than the length of the nerves to the cerebral cortex. **You're hardwired to react before you know you're reacting!**

The thalamus triggers the hypothalamus to release corticotropic-releasing factor (CRF), which stimulates the pituitary gland to release endorphins and adrenocorticotropic hormone (ACTH). Endorphins are neurotransmitters and hormones (known as the body's opiates) that calm the nervous system and relieve pain—the same chemicals that cause "runner's high." ACTH stimulates the adrenal glands (which are on top of your kidneys) to release adrenaline and cortisol.

Interestingly, physical pain signals go directly up the spinal cord and brainstem to the hypothalamus.

PHYSIOLOGICAL RESPONSES TO THE

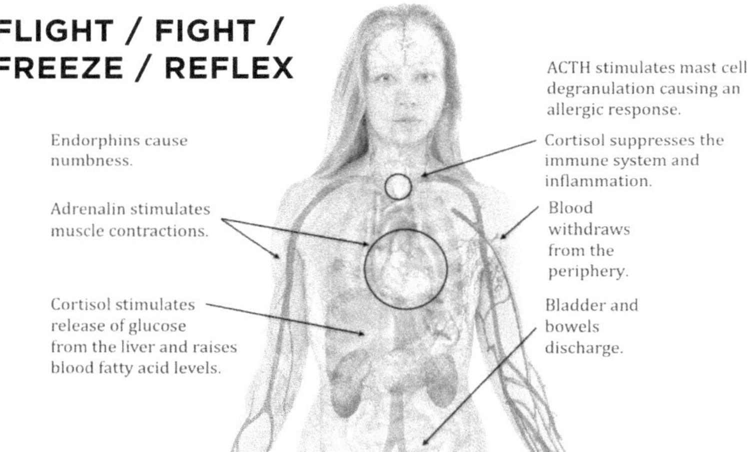

Adrenaline increases the body's ability to perform vigorous muscle activity. It increases arterial pressure so you don't bleed to death or go into cardiac shock. It increases your heart rate and blood flow to active muscles and decreases blood flow to organs such as the gastrointestinal tract and the kidneys that are not needed for rapid motor activity. It doubles the rate of cellular metabolism, increases blood glucose levels, increases muscle strength, and increases mental activity for emergencies: "What do we do now?" An increased rate of blood coagulation needs no explanation.

Cortisol raises blood glucose and fatty acid levels to fuel the muscles and block inflammation by suppressing the immune system. Cortisol lowers fever and increases production of red blood cells.

The bladder and bowels discharge, breathing goes right up into the chest, making it hard to breathe, and the pupils dilate, making your vision fuzzy.

Endorphins cause emotional numbness and suppress physical pain.

This reflex is serious about keeping you alive. The sympathetic nervous system regulates all the functions in the body through a two-nerve system, ***except*** the nerves that go to the adrenal glands. They're the only fibers in the sympathetic nervous system that go direct. What does that tell you? Transmission speed is critical.

The speed of a nerve signal is milliseconds. But when the adrenal glands release a massive dose of adrenaline and cortisol into the circulation, the effects last for minutes, not milliseconds. This reflex is seriously intended to *save your life*.

The Calming Reflex

Remember, for every "on" system in the body, there's an "off" system. Let's look at how the body downregulates the **fight/flight/freeze reflex *(sympathetic alarm response)*** by using the ***calming reflex (stress relaxation response)*** to achieve homeostasis. (In science, this is called feedback regulation.)

Simply put, when the concentration of cortisol and endorphins rises to a high enough level in the bloodstream (about 20 minutes), it shuts off the fight/flight/freeze reflex in the hypothalamus and pituitary (Figure 3). You can only physically panic for about 20 minutes. (This is not comforting to someone having a panic attack, however.)

Endorphins inhibit pain signals, and because pain is a trigger for the stress response, inhibiting pain turns off the trigger. Opioid peptides induce a sense of wellbeing and enhance immune function, counteracting the suppression of the immune system caused by the stress response. Endorphins can also reduce the risk of heart attacks from emotional stress.

THE BODY'S NEUROCHEMICAL RESPONSE TO TRAUMA

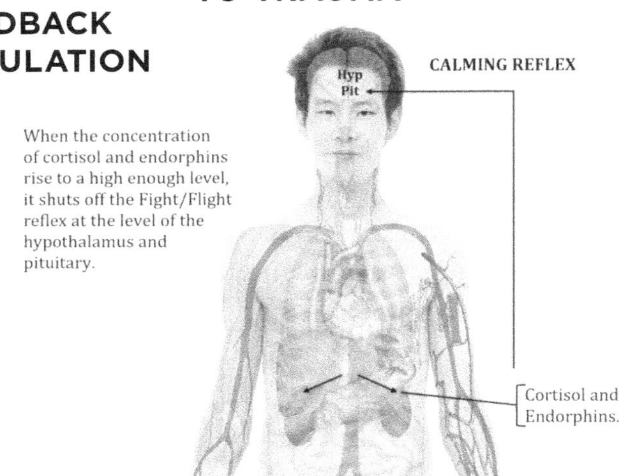

How does tapping on certain areas of the body eliminate phobic reactions? Studies show that stimulating certain acupuncture meridian points *activates the stress relaxation response* (calming reflex) through the release of opioid peptides, thus *inhibiting the sympathetic alarm response* (fight/flight/freeze reflex).

Not surprisingly, all the places we naturally stimulate to calm ourselves correspond to the ends of **acupuncture meridians**. Using NBD or other meridian tapping techniques activates the calming reflex, stimulates the body to release endorphins, downregulates your fight/flight/freeze reflex, and *reconditions* that experience to feel calm!

TAPPING CAN CLEAR ALLERGIC REACTIONS

How does meridian tapping eliminate allergic reactions? Mast cells are the white blood cells that mediate the allergic response. They line every surface of your body to protect you against parasites, and parasites enter through the skin, through the gut, through the linings of your lungs, through the linings of your body.

Mast cells really are there to organize a massive immune effort to kill and digest parasites. Normally, a white blood cell is big enough to engulf and digest a bacterium. But a parasite is a multicellular organism; too big for one white cell to engulf. It requires many white cells surrounding and digesting it to eliminate the parasite.

Mast cells wait in the linings of the body to detect parasites. Mast cells contain granules with signaling molecules to bring in multiples cells to attack the parasite. When a mast cell detects a parasite, it degranulates, i.e., releases the signaling molecules to summon multiple white blood cells to find and attack the parasite.

Allergic reactions are a mistake of the mast cells, which misidentify innocuous substances for parasites. Tree pollen, cat dander, and strawberries are not parasites. Allergies are caused by trauma. Remember, anything that was in the environment at the time you experienced a fight/flight/freeze reaction can act like a trigger for a body flashback, and mast cell degranulation is triggered by the fight/flight/freeze reaction. So, you can develop an allergic reaction to anything that was in the environment at that time. But you can also clear allergic reactions by using NBD to activate the calming reflex!

NERVOUS SYSTEM REGULATION OF MAST CELL DEGRANULATION

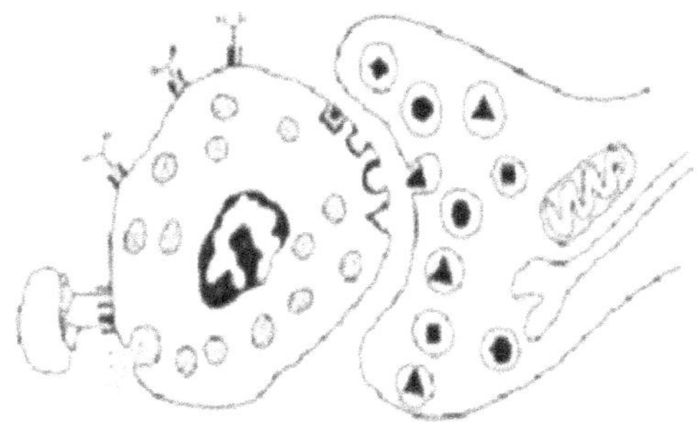

Well, it turns out that mast cell degranulation is stimulated directly by ACTH, triggered by the fight/flight/freeze reflex, and is inhibited directly by endorphins (opioid peptides) from the calming reflex! And, nervous system regulation supersedes immune regulation. In an experiment with mice, pretreatment of experimental animals with opioid peptides followed by allergen challenge prevented anaphylactic shock.

This diagram shows a mast cell and neuron interaction. Normally, in an allergic reaction, the allergen is bound to the antibodies that recognize it. If you've made antibodies against this allergen, the tail of the antibody binds to an Fc receptor on the surface of a mast cell. Allergen binding to two Fc receptors next to each other cross-links the receptors, causing degranulation of the mast cell, thus releasing histamine, inflammatory cytokines, prostaglandins, chemotactic factors, etc. Basically, the soluble factors released through this mechanism are intended to summon a host of white blood cells to devour a *non-existent* parasite.

However, because mast cells are the only white cells in your body that don't circulate—they actually sit down and localize somewhere—*they're directly innervated.* And it turns out that these neurons contain ACTH as their neurotransmitters, and they also contain opioid peptides (although I don't know if the same neuron contains both). *So, there are receptors for both ACTH and opioid peptides regulating the same mast cell.* Studies have shown that if you pretreat mast cells with an opioid peptide and then challenge a mast cell with an allergen, it will prevent degranulation. And that explains why you can often turn off an allergic response immediately using a meridian tapping technique. The release of opioid peptides directly turns off the mast cells.

The original title of my seminar was "Energy Psychology Isn't Weird, It's Biology." And now you know why I don't see anything mysterious or strange about how meridian tapping techniques work. I think this is neurophysiology. So, teach your colleagues, clients, friends, family members, and strangers how to intentionally regulate their own nervous systems using meridian tapping techniques. The world will be a better place.

CHAPTER 7

TREAT TRAUMA BEFORE OR AS SOON AS POSSIBLE

PART 1: THE NATURAL BIO-DESTRESSING TECHNIQUE CAN SAVE LIVES

NBD can be very useful in some physical emergencies. Here are some examples.

Heart Failure

Abby

My family and I went on a vacation to swim with wild dolphins in the Bahamas. Every afternoon, we took a two-hour boat trip out in the open ocean to find them. When we spotted them, we all jumped into the water with our snorkel gear and played with them till they got tired of us and swam away.

The first day out, I talked with Abby, a woman who was interested in mind-body healing and was familiar with Reiki. Abby was 45 years old, 50 to 75 pounds overweight, had lupus erythematosus (an autoimmune disease), and thought she either had asthma or bronchitis; the doctors couldn't decide which. Abby had never snorkeled before.

At the first dolphin sighting, we lined up and jumped into the water. I was on the ladder following Abby into the water when she abruptly came back up. I backed up into the boat, and Abby followed. She was blue-gray and gasping for breath. She grabbed my arm and said, "I'm dying. You're my healer. Save me."

Abby was so out of it that she couldn't even tap on herself. Thinking she was having a panic attack caused by claustrophobia from her snorkel gear, I grabbed her partner. Each of us took one side of her body, and we tapped her for three rounds of NBD. Her breathing returned to normal, and she lay down for the rest of the trip. Abby stayed for the rest of the week, but didn't go snorkeling again. She had shortness of breath. I gave her homeopathy, but she muscle-tested for strange remedies, not the ones for respiratory infections. She saw the island doctor, who gave her oxygen and antibiotics for bronchitis.

Three months later, I called Abby. She said she couldn't believe I had called her that day. She had just returned from a post-operative medical checkup for open-heart surgery! It turned out she suffered from congestive heart failure, and the exertion from snorkeling had put her into heart failure. The tapping had actually saved her life! The day after she returned from the trip, her partner drove her to the emergency room, where they performed an EKG. The next day, she had quadruple bypass surgery!

Allergic Reaction

A colleague

A colleague of mine came running into my lab one day and told me she was breaking out in hives all over her body. "I think it's from something I ate at lunch just now," she said.

"Do you think you're having an anaphylactic (life-threatening) reaction and we should rush you to the hospital?" I asked.

"No," she replied, "I'm just breaking out in hives. They started at my feet and are traveling up my body. They are at my waist now."

I led her through three rounds of Roger Callahan's (originator of Thought Field Therapy) standard trauma tapping sequence, and the reaction stopped. Within an hour, all the hives disappeared.

Roger Callahan himself also reported incidents of using meridian tapping with people who were having anaphylactic reactions. They found that the allergic reactions stopped immediately.

PART 2: THE NATURAL BIO-DESTRESSING TECHNIQUE CAN STOP BLEEDING

It's possible for people who injure themselves to stop the bleeding immediately with NBD. Here are real-life examples of how it works.

Laura

While enjoying dinner at an entertainment restaurant, my daughter, Laura, ran behind some teenagers playing pool. They accidentally backed into her, causing her to trip and fall headfirst into the edge of a bench. She cut her head so badly that she needed five stitches to the muscle inside and seven to the skin outside. It was a serious cut, and she gushed blood. I grabbed a napkin, applied pressure to her head immediately, and screamed for the manager to bring ice, which we applied. While my husband continued to apply pressure, I performed NBD on her, and she stopped bleeding instantly.

We got in the car, performed NBD on ourselves, and calmly drove to the emergency room. The triage nurse looked at Laura's open gash with no blood coming out and taped a piece of gauze over it.

"It's going to be three hours until we can see her, and I don't know how soon we can stitch her after that because we have a lot of people here. You'll just have to wait," she said. Since it wasn't bleeding, there was no hurry.

I said to my husband, "We're going someplace else because I don't like the service here." We called up another hospital just ten minutes away in our own town and asked if the emergency room was busy. It wasn't. We went, and she was stitched in half an hour.

Cathy

The same thing happened when our nanny's friend brought over her two-year-old, Cathy. She sat in her little chair, rocked backwards, knocked her head into the back of a shelf, and cut the back of her head open. Head wounds really gush. So, we applied pressure with a towel, put ice on it, and did a complete round of NBD. Cathy stopped bleeding immediately. We calmly called up the emergency room at the local hospital, told them we were coming, got in the car, and drove there. All the moms tapped while waiting. Cathy needed two stitches on the back of her head.

My Hairdresser

My hairdresser cut her finger with the scissors while she was cutting my hair. I expected that cutting your finger is a regular job hazard for hairdressers, so I wasn't particularly concerned.

She said, "Excuse me, I have to go get a Band-Aid." Then she came back and added, "It's still bleeding, and it's pulsing."

This indicated she was having a traumatic reaction to the cut. So, I led her through a round of NBD, and her finger stopped bleeding.

HOW DOES TAPPING STOP BLEEDING?

I didn't understand why NBD would stop bleeding so fast. Why was it that even with serious gashes, there was no blood after tapping? The famous Norma Feldman figured it out. She told me, "Well, Judith, when they tap, their heart stops pumping so hard." I realized she was right. The opioid receptors feed back directly to the heart to neutralize the pumping.

PART 3. DETRAUMATIZING CHILDREN

THE TWO-TO-THREE-MINUTE LAG TIME

I have found a two-to-three-minute lag time between treatment with NBD and cessation of symptoms (usually crying) in children ages four and under, so don't think it's not working just because your child continues to scream while you tap.

Laura

When Laura was two years old, I took her to the pediatrician for her annual checkup and immunizations. I treated her with NBD before and after her shot. After a couple of minutes, Laura stopped crying and returned to her normal, cheerful self. When I went to pay for the appointment, the receptionist didn't believe Laura had really gotten her shot. She summoned the nurse to confirm it.

Camilla

Three-year-old Camilla and her parents came to our house for dinner one evening. Unfortunately, Camilla fell asleep in the car on the way over, and when her parents arrived, they reluctantly woke her. Camilla screamed inconsolably to be left alone to sleep, but they couldn't just leave her in the car. So I went out to the car and talked to her reassuringly while tapping her at the top of the head (which was all I could reach). I went back in the house, told her parents to wait three minutes, and sure enough, they came back in with a smiling child.

Nightmares

Nightmares are common, but not normal. If children (or grown-ups) have nightmares, it indicates they've been traumatized. In addition to real traumatic events, nightmares in children can be caused by visually scary things, such as TV shows.

Remember that the brain develops the ability to distinguish fantasy from reality after age seven. That's why I don't think it's funny to tell children absurd stories about the boogie man or witches coming to get them, and laugh when the child reacts. I even have mixed feelings about Santa Claus.

Pictures or cartoons of monsters, including Halloween masks, can be really frightening and cause sleeplessness or even nightmares. If the child is an infant and screams in his sleep, tap him in the moment. If the child is older, ask what he saw (or heard) that scared him, and tap on the memory. Then forbid him to watch that TV show or go to a party store at Halloween till he's older.

TREATING PHOBIAS IN CHILDREN UNDER SEVEN

Phobic reactions can be triggered by sights, sounds, feelings, and smells. In adults, it's enough to remember the phobic moment and treat it once; all the triggers in each representational system clear simultaneously. In children under age seven, I found that each phobic trigger must be treated separately and may take several rounds of tapping. I assume the brain hasn't sufficiently developed yet to coordinate the information into a unified whole.

For example, Karen couldn't fall asleep unless her mother lay down beside her (sometimes for more than an hour), and if Karen woke in the middle of the night, she'd have to get her mother to come to bed with her so she could go back to sleep. Her sleep-deprived mother brought Karen in and told me the problem was a phobic reaction caused by watching a scary TV show.

Karen was afraid of being kidnapped. In the movie, a teacher was kidnapped when kidnappers came in through the bedroom window. Her young students followed a trail of clues to rescue her. This included going to a library at midnight. There, they evaded the ghost of a librarian who kept the library silent by capturing people's voices who dared to talk out loud. The voices were kept in a box closed by rattling chains.

Karen's bedroom and hallway both had windows. We focused the first round of tapping on the vision of kidnappers coming through the windows to get her. The second round was to clear the scary sound of the ghost librarian's laugh. The third round was on the sound of the rattling chains on the box. Karen was able to go to sleep by herself from that night on.

Toddlers

Toddlers do understand what you say, even if they don't have the language skills to express themselves. I found that if a toddler talks about a frightening (to them) event for more than 24 hours, they have a trauma. If the parents didn't tap on the child while the traumatic event was happening, they can elicit the memory hypnotically. Hold the child on a parent's lap, do NBD, and talk hypnotically. For example: "Remember the time when _________, and you felt like _________, but now you're okay and everything is fine?"

Laura

We used this approach on Laura when she was 18 months old and needed a head X-ray. Laura had a ridge on her forehead, so my husband and I decided, together with her pediatrician, to have her head X-rayed to make sure the bones weren't closing prematurely and possibly squeezing the brain. I knew the procedure would traumatize Laura, but figured I'd detraumatize her afterward.

While Laura screamed, the X-ray technician held her head still, and I immobilized the rest of her body by lying flat on top of her. After it was over, I held Laura and did NBD while saying, "Remember the time we X-rayed your head and held you down on the table while you screamed? And remember how frightened and angry and betrayed you felt, and how, when it was over, you were really okay? And when the doctor read the X-ray, your head was perfect?"

Interestingly, Laura was tense during the whole tapping sequence until we got to "your head was perfect?" I realized she'd been present during the whole conversation with the doctor, and probably understood enough to feel either worried or insulted that we could possibly think there was anything wrong with her.

CHILDREN THREE TO SEVEN YEARS OLD: USING THE DRAWING TECHNIQUE

I can't usually muscle test children under five and a half years old. They wiggle too much and have trouble paying attention to the questions. In these cases, I usually start by asking the child why she is there to see me. She looks quizzically at her mother, who explains.

I ask the child, "Is that right?" and the child nods. At this point, I ask the child to draw me a picture of the problem. I have a tempting collection of colored, non-toxic markers, a step stool, and a large white flip chart. After they draw the picture, I ask them to explain it to me, which they excitedly do.

I then ask where they feel the negative emotion (fear, frustration, etc.) in their body. They often point to their head. (I don't think they actually feel all their emotions in their heads. I don't believe they understand the concept of what I'm asking.) I then instruct their mother to do NBD with the child. The child then draws another picture until the pictures are neutral or happy.

Jill

Jill was a five-year-old child born with many birth defects. She'd had many operations by the time she was five and was deathly afraid of shots and needles. Her mother, Wanda, brought her to me because Jill needed a tonsillectomy to be able to breathe at night. I asked Jill to draw a picture of the problem. She drew a huge brown needle diagonally across the flip chart paper and a small stick figure human in the lower right corner. When I asked her where she felt the fear in her body, she smiled and pointed to her head.

Her mother did NBD and talked along with me. We said, "Remember all those operations you had when you were little and how frightened you were, and you thought your mother hated you and gave you to the mean doctors to torture you because you thought you were bad? But really, your mother loves you, and the doctors were trying to help you by fixing your body so it worked better and you could be more comfortable? And remember how much it hurt to get shots and surgery, but how fast your body healed and felt much better? And how you need to get your tonsils removed so you can breathe more easily at night, and it will be a small operation, and you will recover very quickly and be happy?"

The second picture was a giant Band-Aid, and she told us how much it hurt to have a Band-Aid removed after a shot. We tapped her again while I said, "The secret to removing a Band-Aid so it doesn't hurt is to pull it off really fast, so it only takes a second and you don't even notice it. Your mother knows how to do that, and will remove all your Band-Aids that way from now on."

The third picture was of a house, a tree, and the sun.

Her mother reported that Jill sailed through her next surgery and recovered well.

I believe that we're all born radiant, happy, loving beings of light. That light begins to tarnish and dim as children experience trauma. As a parent, I decided to do everything in my power to keep my daughter's light bright, so I treated every negative experience or other types of damage patterns as soon as I found them. I also taught her how to treat herself. I have the same intention for my clients of all ages: to clear the tarnish and let their true light shine.

In the next chapter, I share several simple, easy-to-use protocols for treating trauma and optimizing your functioning throughout life's many challenges. Use them!

CHAPTER 8

PROTOCOLS

PROTOCOL 1. THE DO-IT-YOURSELF PROTOCOL FOR TREATING TRAUMA

Whenever a person experiences a major loss (real or imagined) or an episode of violence, they feel a flood of negative emotions and develop a series of limiting beliefs shown in the loss and violence trauma outlines on the following pages. Here are simple directions for clearing trauma.

You can do this protocol with or without muscle testing. You can do it by yourself, with a friend who will listen and talk with you about it while you do it, or with your therapist.

I've muscle-tested clients who use this protocol for themselves and found they cleared all or most of the trauma!

THE SIMPLE 4-STEP TRAUMA CLEARING PROTOCOL

Step 1. Recall a memory where you experienced a trauma.

Step 2. Read the Loss and Violence Trauma Outlines on the next couple of pages and notice which emotions or beliefs show up for you, resonate for you, or jump out at you.

Step 3. Connect with that feeling and treat with Natural Bio-Destressing (NBD).

Step 4. Repeat steps 2 and 3 until there's nothing or very little left that bothers you about the memory, i.e., doesn't trigger any remaining negative reaction.

THE SLIGHTLY MORE SOPHISTICATED TRAUMA CLEARING PROTOCOL

Step 1. Recall a memory where you experienced a trauma.

Step 2. Read the Loss and Violence Trauma Outlines on the next couple of pages and ask yourself: *Does this trauma feel like a loss trauma, a violence trauma, or both?*

Step 3. For a **loss trauma**, ask yourself: *What did I think, feel, or imagine I lost in that moment?*

For a **violence trauma**, ask yourself: *Who was the perpetrator of violence? Is it someone else, something else, or me?*

Step 4. Read whichever trauma outline you're using and notice which emotions or beliefs show up for you, resonate for you, or jump out at you. Notice where in your body you feel this.

Step 5. Connect with that feeling and treat with NBD.

Step 6. Notice that the feeling you were treating has diminished or is gone. If there is still something left, treat again with NBD.

Step 7. Read the trauma outline again. Notice if there are any other feelings or beliefs that show up for you, resonate for you, or jump out at you. Locate the feeling in your body, and treat it with NBD. Repeat this step until there's nothing or very little left that bothers you about the memory.

Note: You can usually clear a whole trauma in two to three rounds of tapping.

Step 8. Write about what you learned. After you clear trauma, which is irrational, you can now access what's true and real. Just write what comes to you from the inside, like automatic writing or stream of consciousness writing. Learnings can be single sentences, phrases, words, feelings, insights, different memories, or different interpretations of the same memory.

Sometimes the learnings indicate that there are still negative emotions or limiting beliefs about the issue, or another trauma or reveals itself. These types of learnings indicate that there is still work to be done on that issue, and this is the next piece of work to treat.

If you or the healing professional you're working with know how to use muscle testing, muscle test the subject through each line of the trauma outline to make sure you've found and cleared every line.

For a Physical Injury Trauma

Each physical injury trauma has physical *and* emotional imprints.

Treat physical injury trauma the same as you would a loss (or occasionally a violence) trauma. On *each line* of the outline, ask if there is any *physical or emotional* __________.

To add another level of depth to the treatment, use muscle testing to check for trauma to all the tissues involved in that experience. I used to use anatomy books, but now I use Google to search for images of body parts and tissues so I can test for all the tissues involved in the injury.

THE NATURAL BIO-DESTRESSING DIAGRAM

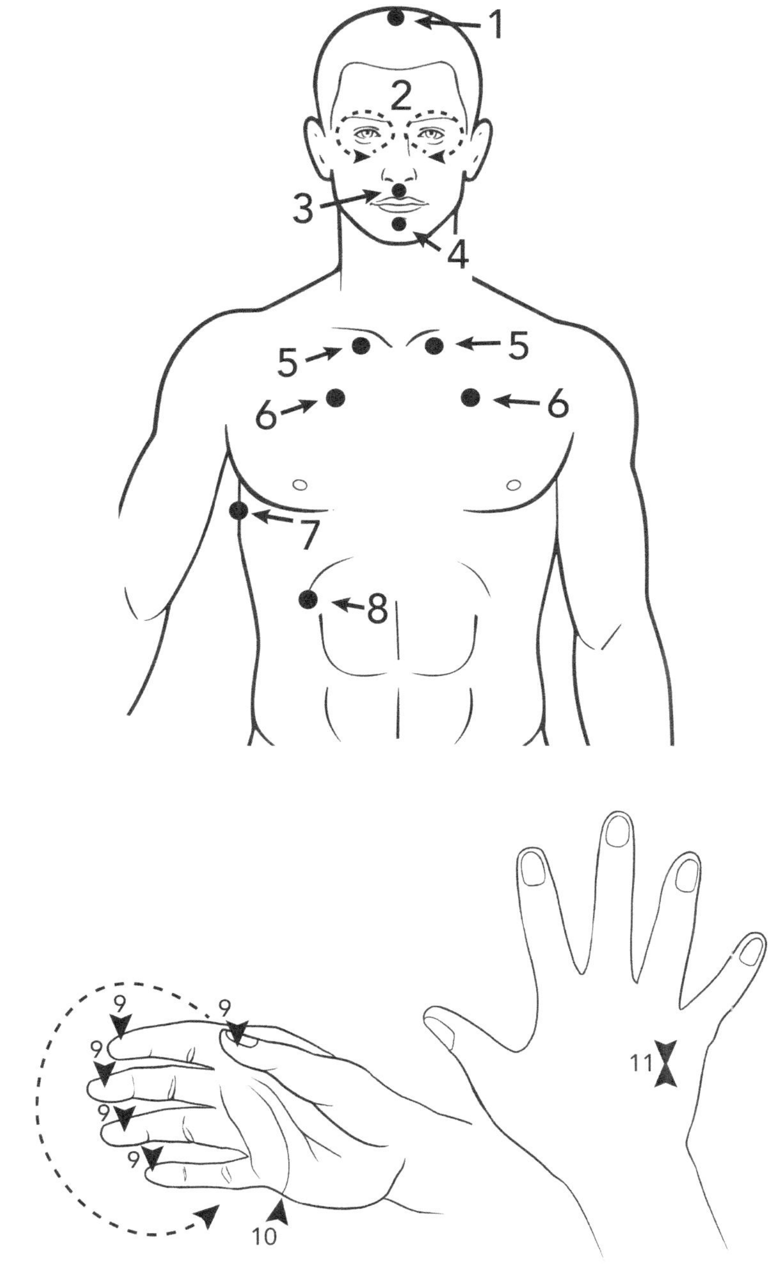

THE NATURAL BIO-DESTRESSING TECHNIQUE (NBD)

A. Concentrate on a specific feeling and notice its location in your body. On a scale of 1-10, rate how severe the feeling is.

B. Tap the karate chop point, #10, while saying three times, "I totally and completely accept myself, even though I have this (problem _________, feeling _________)."

C. Stimulate nerve endings 1-10 by tapping with fingertips for a few seconds. If you feel a lot of energy moving or the scene is changing, stay on that point till the activity plateaus. If nothing happens on a specific point, move to the next one. Use your intuition about how long to stay on a point.

1. Top of the head
2. Around the entire eye socket starting at the eyebrows by the bridge of nose
3. Under nose
4. Under mouth
5. Under collarbone
6. Sore spot on chest (rub gently)
7. Under arm on rib (ouchy spot)
8. Bottom rib below nipple
9. Side of all the fingers by the nail starting with the thumb
10. Karate chop point

D. Do the 9-Gamut

Tap the Gamut point, #11, on back of hand in the indentation between your pinky and ring fingers the whole time while doing the following:

1. Close eyes
2. Open eyes
3. Look down to one side
4. Look down to the other side

5. Roll eyes around in a circle in one direction
6. Roll eyes around in a circle in *the other* direction
7. Hum a tune
8. Count to 40 by 2's
9. Hum a tune

E. Repeat Step C

F. After every round, recheck how severe is the feeling. It should be gone altogether or very low on the scale. Think about what you learned and what feels or seems different about the situation to you now. If the level of that emotion still seems high, notice what ***else*** about the situation makes you feel frightened, angry, sad, etc. Focus on that subject and repeat the process.

BASIC OUTLINE OF LOSS TRAUMA IMPRINTS

How many things did you lose or feel you lost in that trauma? List all the losses and ask if they can all be cleared together.

I. NEGATIVE EMOTIONS
   A. Shock/Fear
   B. Anger/Rage
   C. Sadness/Sorrow
   D. Hurt/Pain

II. LIMITING (CORE) BELIEFS
   A. Responsibility (guilt/shame/blame)
      1. It's my fault because _________.
      2. It's other people's fault because _________.
      3. Disconnection from God. It's God's fault because _________. (How could God let this happen? There is no God.)
   B. Who will take care of me?
   C. People leave me. I can't trust them.
   D. I am powerless or helpless/I have no control.
   E. I am bad/unlovable/unwanted/undeserving/unworthy.

III. FEELING OF EMPTINESS (Loss or Grief)

IV. OPTIONAL
   A. Bitterness/hate/disappointment/loneliness/other negative emotions.
   B. Other limiting beliefs.
   C. Irrational thoughts.
   D. Parts that feel that I'm already dead.
   E. Limiting decisions: I decided to do _________ because of this trauma.
   F. Limiting identities: I am _________ (something negative).
   G. External messages: i.e., someone else saying it's your fault because, or other messages.
   H. Do you need to do amend-making with or forgive yourself, others, or God?
   I. Root Cause: The setup–was there an earlier trauma, grudge, or underlying belief that predisposed you or set you up to incur this trauma?

V. ANTICIPATORY PHOBIAS

VI. Do I need to treat again to clear all the places in mind, body, and life where this imprint has been stored?

BASIC OUTLINE OF VIOLENCE TRAUMA IMPRINTS

Who did you feel perpetrated violence and what did they do that was violent?

Note: Sexual violence, past life, and genealogical/ancestral traumas should only be treated by a professional.

I. NEGATIVE EMOTIONS
- A. Shock/Fear
- B. Anger/Rage
- C. Sadness/Sorrow
- D. Hurt/Pain

II. LIMITING (CORE) BELIEFS
- A. Responsibility (guilt/shame/blame)
  1. It's my fault because __________.
  2. It's other people's fault because __________.
  3. Disconnection from God. It's God's fault because __________. (How could God let this happen? There is no God.)
- B. Safety
  1. My boundaries have been violated or breached.
  2. I don't feel safe/I feel vulnerable.
  3. I am a victim/I am a target.
  4. People/men/women are dangerous and/or crazy.
  5. I don't trust anyone.
  6. I can't receive from anyone.
- C. Power and control issues
  1. I am powerless/helpless. I have no control.
  2. Power is bad.
  3. I am afraid of power (mine and or other people's).
- D. I am bad/unlovable/unwanted/undeserving/unworthy.

III. FEELING OF POLLUTION

IV. OPTIONAL
- A. Bitterness/hate/disappointment/loneliness/other negative emotions.
- B. Other limiting beliefs.
- C. Irrational thoughts.
- D. Parts that feel that I'm already dead.
- E. Limiting decisions: I decided to do __________ because of this trauma.
- F. Limiting identities: I am __________ (something negative).
- G. External messages: i.e., someone else saying it's your fault because, or other messages.
- H. Do you need to do amend making with or forgive yourself, others, or God?
- I. Root cause: The setup–was there an earlier trauma, grudge, or underlying belief that predisposed you or set you up to incur this trauma?

V. ANTICIPATORY PHOBIAS

VI. Do I need to treat again to clear all the places in mind, body, and life where this imprint has been stored?

PROTOCOL 2. SIMPLE CLEARING EXERCISE

Always do the Simple Clearing Exercise before you do any kind of performance so that you're fully present and grounded in the moment. Treat yourself prior to giving a lecture, doing an interview, or playing any kind of sport. My clients and I do this exercise at the beginning of each HBLU™ healing session.

A. Use the Cook's Balance to Ground and Center Yourself: (*This process can be done sitting or standing.*)

1. Cross one leg over the other.
2. With palms facing outward, cross your hands at the wrists and interlock the fingers. Pull your clasped hands upward and rotate outward so that your pinkies are towards the chest, and the thumbs face outward. Hold this position until you feel your energy settle down into your body and you feel grounded.
3. Unfold yourself.
4. Stand with your feet about two feet apart. Touch the fingertips together with relaxed and rounded fingers (making a little tent shape) and hold your joined hands level with your heart until you feel centered.

COOK'S BALANCE

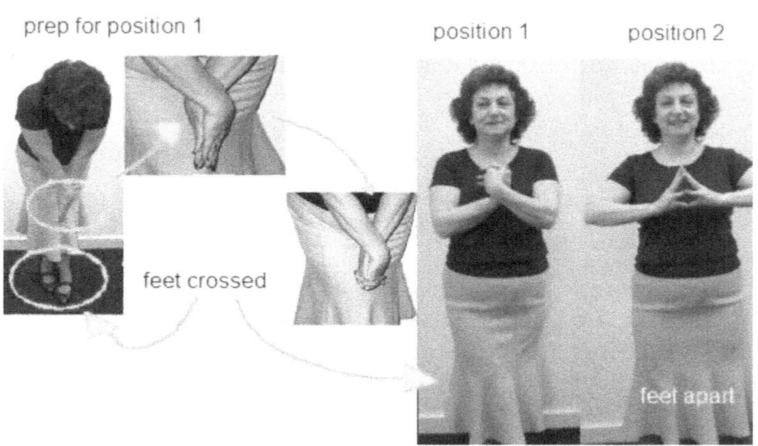

B. Do the Meridian Flush to Energize Yourself: Cup one hand over the other at the bottom of your torso. Make a scooping motion up the center of your body to your lower lip (as if you're splashing yourself with refreshing water). Repeat two to four more times.

MERIDIAN FLUSH

PROTOCOL 3. HBLU™ SUCCESS PROTOCOL FOR FINDING A JOB

Scott

Scott lost his job as an engineer with one of the largest computer companies in the world in one of the many rounds of layoffs that preceded the company's sale. The recruiter he used said he wasn't placing former employees of that company because they were so traumatized that they "acted like losers" at job interviews. Even worse, the company laid Scott off three weeks before Christmas, a time when companies weren't focused on hiring.

Scott came for treatment just one week after he was laid off. We performed the HBLU™ success protocol by clearing his job loss trauma and phobias of failure and then creating a positive vision of the job he wanted next. Lastly, we showed Scott a technique for being fully "on" during job interviews, which he found amazingly helpful. It took just two sessions, and Scott had a new job by February!

MANAGE YOUR EMOTIONAL STATE

When you're looking for a job, it's important to manage your emotional state, particularly your fears. That way, you can keep a positive attitude, stay motivated, and access your ability to be creative and resourceful, a necessity for surviving in hard times. Add the HBLU™ success protocol to the standard procedures for getting a job, i.e., writing a good resume, networking, and searching the job ads, and you'll find a job more quickly and with less anxiety.

I. Clear the Job Loss Trauma

Whenever you experience a job loss, you feel a flood of negative emotions and develop a series of limiting beliefs, standard for any trauma. In order to remain calm, resourceful, and able to rationally deal with whatever needs to be done, follow these directions.

Step 1. Return to the memory where you lost your job. Ask yourself:

- *What was the worst-case scenario I imagined?*

- *Where did I feel the shock in my body?*
- *What did I think, feel, or imagine I lost in that moment?*

Do NBD.

Step 2. Go through the items on the loss trauma outline. Notice which emotions or beliefs show up for you, resonate for you, or jump out at you. *Where in my body do I feel this?*

Do NBD.

Note: Especially with job loss, people imprint the belief that *their work has no value.* Make sure you clear that!

After doing several rounds of NBD, you'll feel calmer, more rational, and better equipped to cope with the situation.

Step 3. As you start your job search, clear phobias of failure.

A. ***Make a list of what you're afraid will happen.*** Remember, a phobia is an exaggerated, irrational emotional (and physical) reaction that's out of proportion with what's happening in reality. ***Fear phobias*** imply an outcome that's life-threatening and ends in some form of death, eternal torment, or rejection. People looking for a job after having to leave their previous position usually have fears about rejection.

Common examples include:

1. *I'll never find a job because of the economy.*
2. *There are no jobs out there in my field.*
3. *I don't really have a chance because I'm competing with too many other qualified applicants.*
4. *I'll be rejected as overqualified, underqualified, or the wrong gender, age, nationality, race, geographic location, etc.*
5. *I'll be rejected for my personality* (too shy, too loud, too independent, for lack of communication skills, etc.).
6. *This isn't a real job opening because they're secretly going to promote someone from the inside, give the job to a friend/relative,* etc.

7. *The company's going to put a freeze on hiring before they can fill this position.*

B. ***Clear the phobias*** by locating the feeling of fear in your body and doing the NBD technique until the fear dissipates (one to three rounds).

C. Write down what you learned while clearing the fears.

II. Focus on the Positive

A. ***Create a wonderful, positive scenario*** of what you would like to have happen in your mind. For example: *They hire me immediately, pay me a great salary, we all get along beautifully, I use all my talents, I make an important contribution to the company, they're glad they hired me, I stay there as long as I want to and continue to progress in my career.*

B. ***Use the Tapas Acupressure Technique*** (TAT) to install your version of a positive outcome in your unconscious mind and body. Hold the bridge of the nose with the thumb and fourth (ring) finger. Place the middle finger on your forehead between the eyebrows (pineal), and place the other hand on the bulge at the back of the head. Do the pose for three minutes while focusing on the positive scenario—what you would like to have happen (1).

C. ***Write down what you learned*** while focusing on the positive, including a list of actions that you will now take.

III. To perform your best, do the Simple Clearing Exercise just before the job interview.

PROTOCOL 4. HBLU™ OPTIMUM SPORTS PERFORMANCE PROTOCOL

Dolores was the captain of her college cross-country running team. For the finals, they would compete with 50 other teams in their division. The team had never finished higher than 30th place in its history.

Before the race, Dolores did TAT step one and cleared her fear that she wouldn't run as well in competition as she could during training. She did TAT step two while imagining, *I run my best race. Everyone on the team runs their best race. We beat our rivals. Our coaches and fans are very proud.*

The day of the race, all Dolores's teammates did the Simple Clearing Exercise (Protocol 2 in this chapter). They finished in 11th place, and for the first time in history, beat their arch-rivals, who finished in 15th place!

Optimum sports performance requires physical skill, hard work, excellent coaching, the right mental attitude and good mind-body integration.

As part of our HBLU™ Sports Performance Program, we teach all our athletes simple but powerful techniques for:

- Maintaining optimum energy, focus, and concentration throughout every game
- Replacing negative self-talk and pictures with convincing positive outcomes

In addition, we treat the following unconscious issues of:

- Performing better in practice than in competition
- Fears of failure or success
- Residual pain, automatic holding back in the body, and incomplete healing from physical injury
- Sabotage from team politics

so our clients can perform their best in every game and at every meet.

Over the years, we have worked with many grateful high school, college, Olympic, and professional athletes.

PROTOCOL

Step 1. Clear all physical injury trauma from the body.

This includes all athletic injuries as well as any other injuries sustained from accidents or illnesses. The physical anticipatory phobias from previous injuries interfere with full range of motion, and injuries from illnesses, especially respiratory illness, interfere with breathing.

Step 2. Clear all emotional trauma from personal and team athletic disappointments or failures.

It's one thing to say, *I'm going to leave the memory of that last game behind and focus on the current game*, and another thing to do it. It's better to clear the trauma and not have old memories affect your current performance. Treat trauma for experiences where you felt you didn't do your best or failed somehow and let your team down, and experiences where other members of your team did the same. This includes the anticipatory phobias that you will make the same mistake or fail again.

Step 3. The week before the event, especially, eat, sleep, and train properly. Each sport has an optimum training regimen that usually requires months if not years of serious and disciplined training. But the week before the event, it's especially important to review and recommit to the training regimen to refresh your sense of focus, dedication, and confidence.

Step 4. Focus on the Positive

One or two days prior to the athletic event, do TAT step one to clear any negative feelings or imaginings about the upcoming event. Do TAT step two to insert the positive representation of what you would like to have happen for yourself and your team.

A. ***Create a wonderful, positive scenario*** of what you would like to have happen in your mind.

B. ***Use TAT*** to install your version of a positive outcome in your unconscious mind and body. Hold the bridge of the nose with the thumb and fourth (ring) finger. Place the middle finger on your forehead between the eyebrows (pineal), and place the other hand on the bulge at the back of the head. Do the pose for three minutes while focusing on the positive scenario, what you would like to have happen (1).

Write down what you learned while focusing on the positive, including a list of actions you will now take.

Step 5. Fifteen minutes to half an hour prior to the event, do the Simple Clearing Exercise (Protocol 2 in this chapter) for yourself (and your teammates if possible).

PROTOCOL 5: SURGERY OR INVASIVE THERAPY PREPARATION PROTOCOL

This protocol is used to *prevent* trauma and stimulate healing from surgery. It can also be used to optimize the effects of other therapies for serious illnesses, such as chemotherapy or radiation.

1. Clear any prior physical injury traumas to that area of the body, including prior surgeries, so the additional treatment won't stack up in the tissues. This includes any prior bad drug reactions from prescription, non-prescription, or illegal drugs (including any kind of chemotherapy).

2. Go inside and explain to your unconscious mind and body that the treatment you're about to receive is a ***healing intervention*** and not a traumatic wounding. Thus, your unconscious mind and body can cooperate fully to optimize the effectiveness of the treatment without traumatizing.

3. **Clear any phobias about the treatment.**

a. Ask: *What is my* ***worst fear pertaining to the treatment***? Locate that fear in the body. Treat with NBD.

b. Get details about the surgery so the body knows what to expect and can be ready to easily handle it. Make sure to ask questions like:

- Will the doctors use a throat tube to help the body breathe during surgery?
- Will there be any transfer of tissues (such as veins from the leg to the heart in bypass surgery)?
- Will there be cooling of the body and/or temporary cessation of breathing (such as the process of being transferred to a heart-lung machine during cardiac surgery)?
- What kind of anesthetic will be used?

c. **Clear anticipatory fear of invasion.**

Bodies never want to be:

- Penetrated, punctured, sliced, or cut, which they equate with being stabbed
- Irradiated, which they equate with being burned
- Treated with chemotherapy, which they equate with being poisoned

Thus, they have a fear of invasion, common for *any* type of treatment.

Locate that fear in the body. Treat with NBD.

4. **Instruct the body to cooperate with and participate in the healing intervention**.

a. For surgery:

While tapping, do a **hypnotic induction**, instructing the body to cooperate with the surgical process. **Add details specific to that particular surgery**.

Tell the subject, "Nod to let me know when the fear of invasion starts to dissolve." When the subject nods, say:

"Now, instruct your body to dose the area with endorphins to prevent pain and shock. Then, remove blood from the area to prevent blood loss and allow a clean field for operating. Relax and cooperate as much as possible to allow the surgeons easy access to the area. After the surgery is done, flood the area with endorphins again to prevent pain, swelling, or scarring. Bring the blood back into the area with oxygen, nutrients, and healing cells to repair the tissue fully. The blood will also bring immune system cells to the area to clean up any cellular debris, to prevent infection, and to promote healing. Your liver will process the anesthetic easily, and you will wake up feeling refreshed and alert."

b. For Chemotherapy or Radiation:

While tapping, do a **hypnotic induction**, instructing the body to cooperate with the treatment process.

Tell the subject, "Nod to let me know when the fear of invasion starts to dissolve." When the subject nods, say:

"Now, instruct your body to direct the healing therapy to the sites where it is needed and can be most effective, and away from areas of the body that don't need and can't use the therapy."

c. For Removal of a Part of the Body:

Fear of loss is common for surgery, where parts of the body are removed.

In cases where the subject will lose a part of their body, tell the subject to "go inside and collect any positive energy, gifts, skills, and memories stored in that tissue and transfer them for storage elsewhere in the body. The remaining tissue becomes an empty husk that is no longer needed, and which you won't miss."

5. **Homeopathy:** Recommend that the subject see a homeopath prior to surgery to determine what remedies would be most effective to promote an easy and complete recovery. My clients often report that their homeopaths recommend Arnica montana (200C), one of the most commonly used remedies for healing bruises and wounds. They recommend the client take arnica a half hour **prior to surgery**. They can stick it under their tongues even if they aren't supposed to eat or drink anything prior to surgery because it's an energy intervention, not food. **After surgery**, they recommend that the client continue to take arnica as soon as he is conscious and as often as necessary to limit pain and promote healing.

6. **Energy Healing:** Follow up surgery or other treatment with energy healing such as Reiki, chi, polarity therapy, therapeutic touch, or other forms of hands-on healing.

7. **Additions to the body:** If there has been an addition to the body such as screws, metal or plastic plates for broken bones, posts in teeth with root canals, etc., **do unwinding/frontal occipital (U/FO holding)* to integrate 100% with gratitude the addition to the body as self.**

8. **Replacements for body parts**: If the surgery involved replacing a part, i.e., heart, kidney, liver, lung, cornea, lens (as in cataract surgery),

bone marrow transplant, breast implant, knees, hips, bone graft, etc., **do U/FO holding* to integrate 100% with gratitude the addition to the body as self.**

*Perform the **U/FO holding** intervention by placing one hand on your forehead and one hand flat across the bulge in the back of your head. Concentrate on the issue you're working on. Your head will move however it wants to and stop automatically.

What to do for people who have had treatment without having done the surgery preparation protocol:

1. Treat the subject for physical injury trauma. The goal statement will usually be something like, "Heal the body part from the surgery."

   a. Muscle test and check for initial shock/fear to the tissue.

   b. **Check whether different tissues have traumatized independently**, i.e., is there any trauma to the muscles, ligaments, tendons, bones, nerves, blood vessels, skin, fascia, organs, etc.?

For example, in open-heart surgery, the heart will shock, but the lungs will shock independently because they're stopped temporarily during transfer to the heart/lung machine. The lungs may imprint a phobia called "I am frozen" or "I have stopped." This may result in the accumulation of fluid in the lungs, pneumonia, or night panic following surgery. The liver may also shock. Treat the trauma imprints with NBD. Check for any additional negative emotions besides shock/fear, and always finish by clearing the anticipatory phobia.

2. If a subject has been injured by a doctor, the client may perceive the doctor as a perpetrator of violence. Treat the surgical trauma like a violence trauma and smudge the feeling of pollution.

3. **Additions to the body:** If there has been an addition to the body, such as screws, metal or plastic plates for broken bones, posts in teeth with root canals, etc., **do U/FO holding to integrate 100% with gratitude for the addition to the body as self.**

4. **Replacements for body parts:** If the surgery involved replacing a part, i.e., heart, kidney, liver, lung, cornea, lens (as in cataract surgery),

bone marrow transplant, breast implant, knees, hips, bone graft, etc. **do U/FO holding to integrate 100% with gratitude the addition to the body as self.**

PROTOCOL 6: MUSCLE TESTING INSTRUCTIONS FOR FACILITATORS AND SUBJECTS *OR* HOW TO AVOID THE COMMON MISTAKES OF MUSCLE TESTING

In an HBLU™ session, the first step is to do the Simple Clearing Protocol to ready the body for muscle testing. I tell people, the body is the lie detector machine, and we start by calibrating the machine. The second step is to establish accurate muscle testing signals so we can communicate with all levels of the being. When I work with people remotely, I teach them self-muscle testing (Protocol 7 in this chapter).

I. Preparation

We start the work by explaining that HBLU™ (and energy psychology in general) works with the conscious mind, unconscious mind, body, and soul simultaneously. In order to do the healing, the person receiving the healing (i.e., the subject) needs to be able to consciously access information from all levels of his being.

1. Accessing the unconscious mind. Teach the subject how he can access his unconscious mind using the NLP technique of going inside and talking to the part that needs healing. The response takes the following forms:
   - Visual: a picture, a memory, a dream you can see.
   - Auditory: a thought in words, a piece of music, a tone of voice.
   - Kinesthetic: a physical or emotional sensation felt in the body. Sometimes there's a taste or smell response.
2. Accessing the body and soul. We teach the subject how to consciously access information from the body and soul levels using an applied kinesiology technique called muscle testing, which is based on the same principle as lie detector testing; that is, the body will register true or false to questions.

3. Once we've established communication with the unconscious mind, body, and soul, **the subject's soul/deepest wisdom dictates all the goals, directions, and healing steps** we do during a session. This includes information about which patterns interfere with the goal, where they're located in the body, and which interventions to use to clear them.

II. Muscle Testing in Yes/No Mode

Explain to the subject, "There are two ways to muscle test, **the easy way**, which is easy, and **the hard way**, which is foolproof." Say, "I prefer the easy way, but I'll show you both so we can decide how we want to do it."

1. "The **easy way to muscle test** is to float your arms out in front of you and let your unconscious mind and body answer automatically. We'll ask your body yes/no, true/false questions. Your conscious mind's job is to send the question into your body, watch the answer your body gives, and *then* think about it. Remember, the sequence is **send the question down, test, think** in that order.

   "The reason we do it this way is that we don't want your conscious mind to answer these questions. If I wanted your conscious answer, I'd ask your face. I'm assuming if the problem were conscious, you would've figured it out by now and not be here in my office.

   "So, we need to communicate with your unconscious mind, body, and soul to find out what else might be happening here. Even if your conscious mind thinks it knows the answer, we still want to know what the other levels of your being have to say. So, your conscious mind is Sherlock Holmes, and I am Watson, and this is HBLU™ Mystery Theater. Our attitude is, 'inquiring minds want to know.' Stay in a state of open-ended scientific curiosity: *I don't know the answer, and I'm interested to find out what the rest of me has to say about the issue.* Even if the question sounds fascinating, and many of them will, send the question straight down into the body rather than holding it in your head and thinking about it.

> "Stay consciously alert while we do the muscle testing. Whether you prefer to keep your eyes open or closed, stay awake and don't space out or go on autopilot. Each question needs to be sent down into your body for evaluation."

To muscle test, the facilitator presses gently on the subject's arms just above the wrists using either the flat palms of the hands or the fingertips. Ask the subject what he prefers. Press until you feel muscle resistance. On a yes, we expect the subject's arms to hold strong (and not move). On a no, we expect the subject's arms to float down all the way to the side of their body without resistance.

Without telling the subject what to expect, ask the subject:

- **"Show me a yes; give me a body yes."** *Muscle test the yes signal.*
- **"Show me a no; give me a body no."** *Muscle test the no signal.*

YES

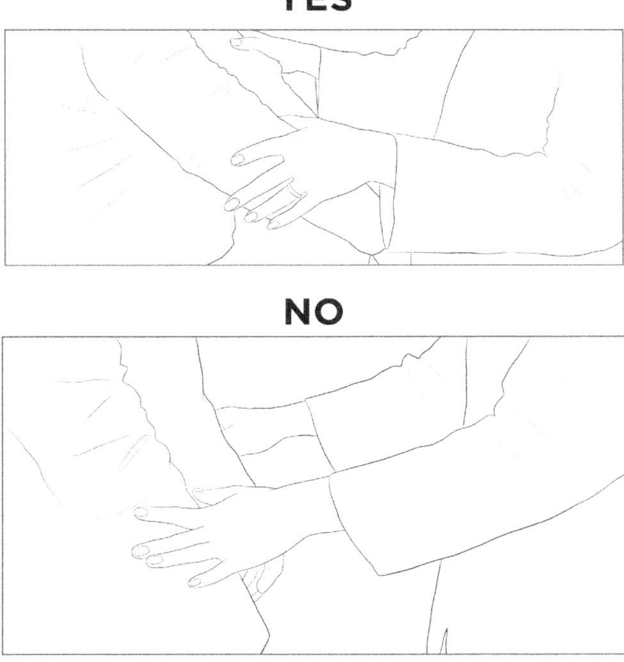

How do you know the subject isn't consciously answering the muscle testing? On an unconscious yes, the arm holds firm. If the conscious mind answers, the arm jerks *up*. On an unconscious no, the arm doesn't move down until the facilitator presses on it. On a conscious no, the subject throws their arms down.

2. "The **hard way to muscle test** is for people who can't let go of conscious control of their body, i.e., the control freaks. In this case, we give the conscious mind something to do consciously in addition to sending the question down.

"We ask you to hold your arm out straight to the side at shoulder height, which takes some effort, and to hold strong *no matter what we ask you.* You still send the question down into your body, observe the answer, and then think about it."

- **"Show me a yes; give me a body yes."** *Muscle test the yes signal.*
- **"Show me a no; give me a body no."** *Muscle test the no signal.*

The facilitator faces the subject squarely, places one hand on the subject's shoulder to stabilize himself, and presses firmly on the subject's arm just above the wrist using the flat palm of the hand. Press until you feel muscle resistance. On a yes, we expect the subject's arms to hold strong (and not move). On a no, we expect the facilitator to be able to press a subject's arm all the way down to their waist while feeling muscle resistance all the way.

How do you know the subject isn't consciously answering the muscle testing? In this position, as long as the subject is consciously holding muscle resistance, he can't consciously influence the answer. Remind the subject periodically to hold his arm strong. If that arm gets tired (isn't holding strong on yes after a while), switch to the other arm.

If the subject can't muscle test the easy way (i.e., rigid on yes and no or controls the muscle testing consciously), or doesn't trust their conscious mind not to interfere, use the hard way. If the subject muscle tests well the easy way, suggest using the easy way, which requires less physical effort.

III. Timing Issues for the Facilitator

Finish asking the question and allow it to register in the subject's body *before* pressing on their arm. Timing: Some subjects register the answer immediately. Others may require a brief pause between questions and testing, and some subjects you may have to count to three before testing. Subjects whose native language is different than the one you're working in may have to translate the question before sending it into their body. Have the subject signal you when the question has registered in his body, then test him.

IV. Unexpected Results

If the subject gives muscle testing signals that are different than what you expect (as described above), go to the muscle testing troubleshooting guide (section VI below) and heal the subject's body and energy field to correct the muscle testing.

Facilitator, do not surrogate muscle-test yourself for the subject and give the subject answers from your body. The subject may begin to suspect that the facilitator is imposing their answers upon him, and doubt that the answers are really coming from within himself. The real work here is to unblock or repair the subject's energy field so he can get real answers from *within himself.*

V. Muscle Testing in Indicator Mode

For counting lists or numbers of things, we switch into Indicator Mode. Say to the subject, "In indicator mode, your arms hold strong while we count and go down when we get the right number. Then, we'll double-check the answer in yes/no mode."

Then, state the question as follows: "In indicator mode, how many __________ (example: traumas do you have on this goal?)" and then start counting.

Other examples:

- "This trauma occurred at what age, going for indicator, between conception to birth, 0-10 years old, 11- 20 years old, 21-30 years old …"

- "What is the priority intervention to use, going for indicator, 1, 2, 3, 4, 5…"

Until the subject is familiar with switching modes, during the first few sessions, remember to look them in the eye while saying, "In indicator mode…" and wait until they nod to let you know they've switched modes.

Then say, "double checking with yes/no…," look the subject in the eye, and wait till they nod to let you know they've switched back into yes/no mode.

Here are a few handy tips for keeping yes/no and indicator modes distinct. Some of our colleagues like to say, "In indicator mode, *counting* 1, 2, 3, etc." Others prefer, "Drop to indicate, 1, 2, 3, etc."

Never say, "Going for indicator *is it* 1, 2, 3, etc." "Is it" is a yes/no question, and mixes the two modes, creating confusion.

VI. Muscle Testing Troubleshooting Guide

1. The subject tests ***strong*** on **yes** and ***strong*** on **no**. This result means the energy field is blocked. Say to the subject, "You have a blocked energy field. This is caused by one or more phobias. It can be difficult to function when your energy field is blocked, so let's clear it now." The subject agrees. Do the **Unblocking Procedure** (step 7 below).

Note: I have had several clients for whom it took three or four sessions of tapping to unblock their energy fields.

2. The subject tests ***strong*** on **yes** and ***tense or sticky*** on **no**. This result means the energy field is partially blocked. Say to the subject, "You have a partially blocked energy field. This is caused by one or more phobias. It can be difficult to function when your energy field is blocked, so let's clear it now." The subject agrees. Do the **Unblocking Procedure** (step 7 below).
3. The subject tests ***strong*** on **yes** and ***stronger*** on **no**. This result means the energy field is blocked. Say to the subject, "You have a blocked energy field. This is caused by one or more phobias. It can be difficult to function when your energy field is blocked, so let's

clear it now." The subject agrees. Do the **Unblocking Procedure** (step 7 below).

Note: This type of testing can mean the subject has a phobia of saying "no" or a phobia of weakness. Ask the subject, "Do you recognize that as a problem in your life?" and discuss. If that's the issue, word the phobia, "I'm afraid to say no because..." or "I'm afraid to feel weak because..."

4. The subject tests ***weak*** on **yes** and ***strong*** on **no**. Say to the subject, "This result means you have a limiting belief that's affecting you strongly. A limiting belief is a one-sentence structure you feel is true, even though it is not true, i.e., you believe the opposite of what is true. This is called a reversal. What's the limiting belief that comes up for you now?"

   Have the **subject speak the limiting belief and locate it in the body. Treat the reversal with Natural Bio-Destressing** because *these kinds of reversals are actually phobias*. Retest the client, and if he now muscle tests normally, i.e., strong on yes and weak on no, muscle test and ask if there are any remaining blocks or partial blockages in his energy field. If yes, treat all the phobias until he tests that his energy field is completely unblocked.

5. The subject tests ***weak*** on **yes** and ***weak*** on **no**. It could be **low blood sugar** or malnutrition. Ask the subject: "When was the last time you ate?" If it was several hours ago, **feed the client** a beverage with sugar or a starchy snack. If the person has an eating disorder, discuss the eating disorder and tell her it will be the first thing we treat. Tell her she must eat more the week before she comes in because her body is too weak to muscle test.

6. The subject tests ***weak*** on **yes** and ***weak*** on **no**. If it isn't low blood sugar, then the energy field is blown out. The reaction you are experiencing is so strong, it's like you have a short circuit in your electrical field. Say to the subject, "You have a blown energy field. This is caused by one or more phobias that caused you to blow a fuse. It can be difficult to function when your energy field is blown, so let's turn the circuit breaker back on." The client agrees. **Do the Unblocking Procedure.**

SPECIAL CASE EXAMPLE I

A client tested **weak on yes** and **weak on no**; the fear was located in her solar plexus. When asked what the fear was, she said there was nothing there; she was blank. I took her answer at face value; there was nothing in the solar plexus.

Since the solar plexus is the will center, I concluded that it was telling us she had no will of her own. Angrily, I said, "Yes and no are irrelevant if you have no will of your own. Who did this to you?"

She replied, "I don't know. My father?"

I said, "Let's test that." She stood up and muscle tested beautifully strong on yes and weak on no, and confirmed by muscle testing that her father had taken away her will. In that instant, she decided to take her will back!

SPECIAL CASE EXAMPLE II

A client tested **weak on yes** and **weak on no**. He seemed unable to lift his arms. I asked him why he was so passive. "What traumatized you so badly that you can't even lift your arms?"

He replied, "During divorce proceedings, my ex-wife threatened to take away my children." Although he got joint custody, he hadn't been the same since. I told him it was time to get his power back. He immediately lifted his arms and muscle tested accurately!

THE MORAL OF THE STORY

The first step of HBLU™ is to access the subject's deepest wisdom through muscle testing. Assume if you get anything other than strong on yes and weak on no, *the subject is showing you something* important about himself *that needs immediate healing!* This troubleshooting guide is meant to help you figure out what you're seeing.

If the subject is doing something other than the common examples in this guide, use your intuition, powers of observation, and your subject's insights and guesses to figure out what they're showing you, and treat it. Remember, the unblocking process itself is tremendously healing and may even take three to four sessions to complete.

VII. Unblocking Procedure

1. Write the goal as follows: "Unblock the field."
2. Have the subject read the Introduction to Phobias and Traumas (Chapter 2).
3. Ask the subject to do a head-to-foot scan (I call it an emotional CAT scan) and **locate the phobia blocking the energy field**. Explain that the phobia may feel like anxiety, fear, or nervous energy in his body.
4. **Talk to the phobia** and have it say what it's afraid of. Since it's a phobia, make sure the wording sounds extreme, exaggerated, and irrational. Remind the subject that a fear phobia ends in death, eternal torment, or rejection, and a shame phobia ends in an insult that feels like a slap in the face.
5. **Treat the phobia with Natural Bio-Destressing.**
6. **Retest** the subject. If the muscle testing is still off, map and clear the next phobia(s) until he muscle tests normally, i.e., strong on yes and weak on no. Then muscle test and ask if there are any remaining blocks or partial blockages in his energy field. If yes, treat all the remaining phobias until his energy field tests as completely unblocked.

PROTOCOL 7: SELF-MUSCLE TESTING

The following self-muscle testing techniques can be used when you are muscle testing yourself. Clients I work with remotely self-muscle test while I ask the questions. I found the Standing Tilt Test to be the most accurate form of self-muscle testing, but try the following techniques and find the one that works best for you.

Note: The same patterns that cause confusing muscle testing signals described in the troubleshooting section also apply to self-muscle testing.

1. **Standing Tilt Test:**
    a. Stand up and face North.
    b. Relax your whole body, particularly around the ankles.
    c. Yes = tilt forward (North).
    d. No = tilt back (South).
2. **Circle and Press:**
    a. Make a circle with the thumb and ring finger of your non-dominant hand.
    b. Insert the thumb and index fingers of the other hand into this circle from the bottom.
    c. Hold light tension in the circle.
    d. As you ask questions, press the fingers inserted into the circle outward.
    e. Yes = the circle stays closed and holds the press fingers inside.
    f. No = the circle opens.
3. **Circle and Point:**
    a. Make a circle with the thumb and ring finger of your non-dominant hand.
    b. Insert the index finger of the other hand into the circle from either the top or bottom.
    c. Hold light tension in the circle.
    d. As you ask questions, pull the index finger and circle apart.
    e. Yes = the circle stays closed and holds the index pointer inside.
    f. No = the circle allows the index pointer to pull out.

4. Finger Rubbing:

a. Lightly touch the pads of the index finger and thumb of one hand together.

b. As you ask questions, lightly slide the pads across each other.

c. Yes = the pads slide very smoothly; there is no resistance.

d. No = the pads are sticky against each other; there is resistance.

e. This can also be done using both hands rubbed against each other.

5. One-Handed:

a. Place the pad of the middle finger of one hand on the top of the nail of the index finger on the same hand.

b. The index finger is straight with the middle finger bending to touch it.

c. As you ask questions, press down on the index finger with the middle finger.

d. Yes = the index finger stays straight.

e. No = the index finger bends downward.

6. Leg Testing:

a. Place one ankle on the top of the opposite thigh at the knee.

b. Place both hands against the back of the calf of the top leg.

c. As you ask questions, press the top leg away from you.

d. Yes = the top leg stays on the thigh of the bottom leg.

e. No = the top leg falls off the thigh of the bottom leg.

IN CONCLUSION

I have devoted my life to helping people get unstuck by clearing unconscious self-sabotage so they can create their best life possible. I have found that trauma is the most common pattern that interferes with quality of life. I can't emphasize enough the importance of being able to recognize trauma in its many forms and the ability to rapidly and effectively clear trauma from the mind and body.

By sharing my original research on the structure of trauma and my simple protocols for clearing it, I hope that you'll use what you've learned to stay as trauma-free as possible. May you create the life you desire with the greatest of ease and a minimum of suffering.

Blessings,

Judith A. Swack, Ph.D.

GLOSSARY OF TERMS

APPLIED KINESIOLOGY

A diagnostic system that uses muscle testing to evaluate the body's structural, chemical, and emotional functions. Practitioners interpret muscle strength or weakness to guide treatment decisions.

BIOFIELD

A term describing the field of energy and information that surrounds and interpenetrates the human body. It is believed to influence physical, emotional, and mental health.

CHAKRAS

Energy centers within the body, originating from ancient Indian traditions. Each of the seven primary chakras corresponds to specific physical, emotional, and spiritual aspects of well-being.

CRANIOSACRAL THERAPY

A gentle, hands-on technique that focuses on releasing tensions in the craniosacral system—the membranes and fluids surrounding the brain and spinal cord—to enhance the body's natural healing processes.

EMOTIONAL FREEDOM TECHNIQUE (EFT)

An energy psychology technique that is a form of psychological acupressure that involves tapping on specific meridian points while focusing on emotional distress, with the goal of reducing anxiety, trauma, and negative emotions.

ENNEAGRAM

A personality system that categorizes human behavior into nine core types, each with its own patterns of thinking, feeling, and acting. It is used for personal growth and insight into interpersonal dynamics.

ENERGY PSYCHOLOGY

An umbrella term for mind-body approaches that use techniques involving the human energy system (such as meridians and chakras) to treat psychological conditions and emotional distress.

EYE MOVEMENT DESENSITIZATION AND REPROCESSING (EMDR)

A psychotherapy technique that uses bilateral stimulation, such as guided eye movements, to help individuals process and reduce the distress associated with traumatic memories.

HEALING FROM THE BODY LEVEL UP™ (HBLU™)

A holistic therapeutic methodology developed by Dr. Judith Swack that integrates muscle testing, energy psychology, and neuro-linguistic programming to identify and resolve unconscious blocks to healing.

MERIDIANS

Energy pathways in traditional Chinese medicine through which life force (qi or chi) flows. They are foundational to practices like acupuncture, acupressure, and meridian tapping techniques.

MUSCLE TESTING

Also known as manual muscle testing or applied kinesiology, this technique assesses the body's response to specific stimuli or questions by observing changes in muscle strength.

NATURAL BIO-DESTRESSING (NBD)

Dr. Swack's name for an Energy Psychology technique that is a form of psychological acupressure that involves tapping on specific meridian points while focusing on emotional distress, with the goal of reducing anxiety, trauma, and negative emotions. The instructions for doing this technique are described in Chapter 8 of this book.

NEURO-LINGUISTIC PROGRAMMING (NLP)

A psychological approach that explores the connections between neurological processes, language, and behavioral patterns. It is used for therapeutic change, communication enhancement, and personal development.

POLARITY THERAPY

An integrative approach to healing that balances the body's energy through touch, movement, diet, and self-awareness, based on the concept of positive and negative energy flows.

TAPAS ACUPRESSURE TECHNIQUE (TAT)

A mind-body process developed by Tapas Fleming that combines gentle acupressure on the head with specific self-reflective statements to clear trauma, stress, and limiting beliefs. Do the TAT pose by holding the bridge of the nose with the thumb and fourth (ring) finger. Place the middle finger on your forehead between the eyebrows (pineal), and place the other hand on the bulge at the back of the head. Do the pose for approximately three minutes.

THOUGHT FIELD THERAPY (TFT)

An energy psychology method developed by Dr. Roger Callahan that uses specific tapping sequences on meridian points to relieve emotional distress and psychological symptoms.

TRANSFORMATIVE WHOLISTIC REINTEGRATION (TWR)

A body-mind integration process developed by Dr. Daniel Benor that aims to resolve trauma, stress, and limiting patterns by combining energy techniques, somatic awareness, and emotional processing. Do TWR by crossing your arms across your chest so that your hands rest on your biceps and tap alternately on each arm for approximately 3 minutes.

UNWINDING FRONTAL/OCCIPITAL (U/FO HOLDING)

A hands-on technique in which the practitioner gently holds the client's forehead and back of the head to facilitate emotional release, neurological balance, and cognitive clarity. Perform the **U/FO holding** intervention by placing one hand on your forehead and one hand flat across the bulge in the back of your head. Concentrate on the issue you're working on. Your head will move however it wants to and stop automatically.

NOTES

PROLOGUE

1. Callahan, R. (1985) *5 Minute Phobia Cure: Dr. Callahan's Treatment for Fears, Phobias, and Self-Sabotage.*
2. Swack, J. A. (1994). "The Basic Structure of Loss and Violence Trauma Imprints." *Anchor Point Magazine, 3*(3), 3–23. www.hblu.org
3. van der Kolk, B. A. (2014). *The Body Keeps the Score: Brain, Mind, and Body in the Healing of Trauma*. Viking.
4. Extensive list of research studies on the efficacy of Energy Psychology methods: https://www.energypsych.org/researchdb8c71b7
5. Shapiro, F. (1989). "Efficacy of the eye movement desensitization procedure in the treatment of traumatic memories." *Journal of Traumatic Stress, 2*(2), 199–223.
6. I still work with clients. Here is a list of other HBLU™ trained practitioners: https://www.hblu.org/hblu-practitioners
7. Find an Energy Psychology trained practitioner on this website: https://www.energypsych.org/practitioner-directory

CHAPTER 2.

The Basic Structure of Loss and Violence Trauma

1. Swack, J. A. (1994). "The Basic Structure of Loss and Violence Trauma Imprints." *Anchor Point Magazine, 3*(3), 3–23. www.hblu.org
2. Swack, J. A. (1992). "A study of initial response and reversion rates of subjects treated with the allergy technique." *Anchor Point, 6*(3), 1–10. www.hblu.org

3. Kushner, H. S. (1981). *When Bad Things Happen to Good People.* Schocken Books.

4. Swack, J. A. (2001). "Healing from the Body Level Up™." In F. P. Gallo (Ed.), *Energy psychology in psychotherapy.* New York, NY: W. W. Norton.

5. Swack, J. A. "Healing the Deathwish Pattern." https://www.hblu.org/product/Healing-the-Deathwish-Pattern

6. Swack, J. A. (2009, September). "Elimination of post-traumatic stress disorder (PTSD) and other psychiatric symptoms in a disabled Vietnam veteran with traumatic brain injuries (TBI) in just six sessions using Healing from the Body Level Up™ methodology, an energy psychology approach." *International Journal of Healing and Caring, 9*(3). http://www.ijhc.org and www.hblu.org

7. Swack, J. A. (2012, September). "Elimination of PTSD and psychiatric symptoms in one to six sessions in two civilian women and one female Iraq War veteran using Healing from the Body Level Up™ (HBLU™) methodology, an energy psychology approach." I*nternational Journal of Healing and Caring, 12*(3). http://www.ijhc.org and www.hblu.org

8. Swack, J. A., & Rawlings, W. (2017, November). "Understanding neurobiology of trauma will enable counselors to help clients heal permanently from it." *AMHCA The Advocate Magazine, 40*(4), 9–12. Also at www.hblu.org

CHAPTER 4.

Specific Types of Loss Part 1 Diagnosis Shock

1. Maguire, P. (1994). "ABC of Breast Diseases: Psychological aspects." *BMJ, 309*, 1649–1652.

2. Schuth, W., Karck, U., Wilhelm, C., & Reisch, S. (1994). "Parents' needs after ultrasound diagnosis of a fetal malformation: An empirical deficit analysis." *Ultrasound in Obstetrics & Gynecology, 4*(2), 124.

3. Liefooghe, R., Michiels, N., Habib, S., Moran, M. B., & De Muynck, A. (1995). "Perception and social consequences of tuberculosis: A

focus group study of tuberculosis patients in Sialkot, Pakistan." *Social Science & Medicine, 41*(12), 1685–1692.

4. McDaniel, J. S., Musselman, D. L., Porter, M. R., Reed, D. A., & Nemeroff, C. B. (1995). "Depression in patients with cancer: Diagnosis, biology, and treatment." *Archives of General Psychiatry, 52*, 89–99.
5. Slijper, F. M., van Teunenbroek, A., de Muinck Keizer-Schrama, S. M., & Sas, T. C. (1998). ["A daughter with Turner's syndrome: The impact on parents"] [Article in Dutch]. *Nederlands Tijdschrift voor Geneeskunde, 142*(39), 2150–2154.
6. Gray, R. E., Fitch, M. I., Phillips, C., Labrecque, M., & Klotz, L. (1999). "Presurgery experiences of prostate cancer patients and their spouses." *Cancer Practice, 7*(3), 130.
7. Harcourt, D., Rumsey, N., & Ambler, N. (1999). "Same-day diagnosis of symptomatic breast problems: Psychological impact and coping strategies." *Psychology, Health & Medicine*.
8. Mekarski, J. E. (1999). "Stages of adjustment to a medical diagnosis of a serious somatic condition." *European Psychiatry, 14*(1), 49–51.
9. Osowiecki, D. M., & Compas, B. E. (1999). "Prospective study of coping, perceived control, and psychological adaptation." *Cognitive Therapy and Research, 23*(2), 169–180.
10. Slijper, F. M. E., Frets, P. G., Boehmer, A. L. M., Drop, S. L. S., & Niermeijer, M. F. (2000). "Androgen insensitivity syndrome (AIS): Emotional reactions of parents and adult patients to the clinical diagnosis of AIS and its confirmation by androgen receptor gene mutation analysis." *Hormone Research, 53*(1), 9–15.
11. Chippindale, S., & French, L. (2001). "HIV counseling and the psychosocial management of patients with HIV or AIDS." *BMJ, 322*, 1533–1535.
12. Greer, S. (2002). "Psychological intervention—The gap between research and practice." *Acta Oncologica, 41*(3), 238–243.

13. White, C. A., & Macleod, U. (2002). "Clinical review, ABC of psychological medicine: Cancer." *BMJ, 325*, 377–380.

14. Edwards, B., & Clarke, V. (2003). "The psychological impact of a cancer diagnosis on families: The influence of family functioning and patients' illness characteristics on depression and anxiety." *Psycho-Oncology, 13*(8), 562–576.

15. Fukui, S., & Ozawa, H. (2003). ["Relation of psychological distress after diagnosis of gastric cancer at a cancer screening center with psychological support from public health nurses and family members."] [Article in Japanese]. *Nippon Koshu Eisei Zasshi, 50*(7), 583–593.

16. Rakovitch, E., Franssen, E., Kim, J., Ackerman, I., Pigno, J.-P., Paszat, L., Pritchard, K. I., Ho, C., & Redelmeier, D. A. (2003). "A comparison of risk perception and psychological morbidity in women with ductal carcinoma in situ and early invasive breast cancer." *Breast Cancer Research and Treatment, 77*(3), 285–293.

17. Connell, C. M., Boise, L., Stuckey, J. C., Holmes, S. B., & Hudson, M. L. (2004). "Attitudes toward the diagnosis and disclosure of dementia among family caregivers and primary care physicians." *The Gerontologist, 44*, 500–507.

18. Read, C. Y. (2004). "Using the Impact of Event Scale to evaluate psychological response to being a phenylketonuria gene carrier." *Journal of Genetic Counseling, 13*(3), 207–219.

19. Rispoli, A., Pavone, I., Bongini, B., Di Loro, B., Ponchietti, C., & Rizzo, M. (2005). "Genitourinary cancer: Psychological assessment and gender differences." *Urologia Internationalis, 74*, 246–249.

20. Williams, R. (2005). "Breaking the news. Interview with Estela Beale, M.D." *OncoLog, 50*(10).

21. Swack, J. A. (2001). "Healing from the Body Level Up™." In F. P. Gallo (Ed.), *Energy psychology in psychotherapy*. New York, NY: W. W. Norton.

22. Swack, J. A. (2001). "The biochemistry of energy psychology: An immunologist's perspective on physiological mechanisms underlying energy psychology treatments." Plenary speech presented at the 2001 Energy Psychology Conference. www.hblu.org

23. Swack, J. A. (1994). "The Basic Structure of Loss and Violence Trauma Imprints." *Anchor Point Magazine, 3*(3), 3–23. www.hblu.org

24. Arenson, G. (2001). *Five Simple Steps to Emotional Healing: The Last Self-Help Book You Will Ever Need*. New York, NY: Fireside/Simon & Schuster.

25. Callahan, R. (2000). *Stop the Nightmares of Trauma*. North Carolina: Professional Press.

26. Callahan, R. (2001). *Tapping the Healer Within*. Illinois: Contemporary Books.

27. Durlacher, J. V. (1994). *Freedom from Fear Forever*. Tempe, AZ: Van Ness Publishing Co.

28. Eden, D. (1998). *Energy Medicine: Balance Your Body's Energies for Optimum Health, Joy, and Vitality*. New York, NY: Jeremy P. Tarcher/Putnam.

29. Tapas Fleming's *The Tapas Acupressure Technique* described at https://tatlife.com/

30. Gallo, F. P. (1999). *Energy psychology: Explorations at the Interface of Energy, Cognition, Behavior, and Health*. Boca Raton, FL: CRC Press.

31. Lambrou, P., & Pratt, G. (2000). *Instant Emotional Healing: Acupressure for the Emotions*. New York, NY: Broadway Books.

32. Swack, J. A. (2001). "Clear Trauma Now with Natural Bio-Destressing." Video available at www.hblu.org

33. Swack, J. A. (2008). "Diagnosis shock: The unrecognized burden of illness." *International Journal of Healing and Caring, 8*(1). http://www.IJHC.org or reprint or forward the article to as many people as possible from my website https://www.hblu.org/diagnosis-shock-the-unrecognized-burden-of-illness

34. Daniel Benor's *Transformative Wholistic Reintegration* (TWR) method described at https://www.danielbenor.com/twr-method

35. Norman, Marc. "Doctors Learn How to Say What No One Wants to Hear." *The New York Times*, 10 Jan. 2006.

CHAPTER 6.

The Biochemistry of Energy Psychology: An Immunologist's Perspective on Physiological Mechanisms Underlying Energy Psychology Treatments

Excerpted from the Plenary Address presented by Judith Swack, Ph.D. at the 2001 Conference of the Association for Comprehensive Energy Psychology, (ACEP)

1. Callahan, R. (1985) *5 Minute Phobia Cure: Dr. Callahan's Treatment for Fears, Phobias, and Self-Sabotage.*

2. Lane, J. R. (2009). "The neurochemistry of counterconditioning: Acupressure desensitization in psychotherapy." *Energy Psychology: Theory, Research, and Treatment*, 1(1), 31–44.

3. Church, D., Yount, G., & Brooks, A. J. (2012). "The effect of Emotional Freedom Techniques (EFT) on stress biochemistry: A randomized controlled trial." *The Journal of Nervous and Mental Disease, 200*(10), 891–896.

4. Stapleton, P., Chatwin, H., & Sheldon, T. (2020). "A randomized trial of Emotional Freedom Techniques (EFT) for psychological and physiological symptoms of stress: Cortisol, heart rate, heart rate variability and subjective assessments of stress after a single session." *Psychological Trauma: Theory, Research, Practice, and Policy, 12*(2), 140–147.

5. Feinstein, D. (2019). "Energy psychology: Efficacy, speed, mechanisms." *Explore: The Journal of Science and Healing*, 15(5), 340–351.

6. Guyton, A. C., & Hall, J. E. (2000). *Textbook of Medical Physiology* (10th ed.). W.B. Saunders Co.

7. Ulett, G. A. (1992). *Beyond Yin and Yang: How Acupuncture Really Works*. Warren S. Green and Co., Inc.

8. Stefano, G. B., Fricchione, G. L., Slingsby, B. T., & Benson, H. (2001). "The placebo effect and relaxation response: Neural processes and their coupling to constitutive nitric oxide." *Brain Research Reviews, 35*(1), 1–19.

9. Swack, J. A. (1992). "A study of initial response and reversion rates of subjects treated with the allergy technique." *Anchor Point, 6*(3), 1–10.

CHAPTER 8.

Protocols

Protocol 2: The HBLU™ Success Protocol for Finding a Job and Protocol
Protocol 3: HBLU™ Optimum Sports Performance Protocol

1. Tapas Fleming's *The Tapas Acupressure Technique* described at https://tatlife.com/

   https://hblu.org/

WAS THE INFORMATION IN THIS BOOK HELPFUL TO YOU?

WOULD YOU LIKE TO TAKE THIS WORK TO THE NEXT LEVEL?

COME TRAIN WITH ME!

Register for HBLU™ Module 1: Clearing Trauma and Healing PTSD, and learn to heal trauma professionally. This course is available for mental health and other healing professionals, as well as people who want to use it on themselves, their family members, and friends.

Do you have more complex trauma than is covered in this book, or other problems that you think Healing from the Body Level Up™ could help you with?

My HBLU™-trained colleagues and I are available to do private sessions.

Contact me at info@hblu.org to schedule a free 15-minute consult.

Find other HBLU™-trained practitioners near you at:

https://www.hblu.org/hblu-practitioners

WOULD YOU LIKE TO INTRODUCE MORE PEOPLE TO THIS WORK?

Hire me to speak to your organization.

I'm available to do anything from one-hour presentations to full two-day trainings in person or online.

Email info@hblu.org

ABOUT THE AUTHOR

Judith A. Swack, Ph.D., biochemist/immunologist, Master NLP practitioner, mind-body healer, and best-selling author, is the originator of Healing from the Body Level Up™ (HBLU™), an innovative and powerful methodology with transformative results. HBLU™ integrates biomedical science, psychology, hypnosis, Neuro Linguistic Programming, applied kinesiology, energy psychology, and spiritual techniques with original research on the structure of complex damage patterns. This powerful and effective healing system helps people get unstuck and eliminate struggle by clearing mental, emotional, physical, and spiritual blocks to success.

Dr. Swack has presented her dramatic results live on national television and at international conferences and has published numerous articles in scientific, professional, and popular books and journals. She is a recipient of the 2015 Association for Comprehensive Energy Psychology (ACEP) award for major contribution to the field of energy psychology. Dr. Swack works with clients in person and by Zoom.

Healing from the Body Level Up, Inc.

56 Pickering St., Needham, MA 02492

781-444-6940

https://hblu.org/

www.ingramcontent.com/pod-product-compliance
Lightning Source LLC
Chambersburg PA
CBHW061743120626
46550CB00005B/1876

* 9 7 8 1 9 6 1 4 9 3 8 4 1 *